PENGUIN BOOKS

LUCK OF THE DEVIL

Ian Kershaw was Professor of Modern History at the University of Sheffield from 1989 to 2008. For services to history he was given the German Award of the Federal Cross of Merit in 1994. He was knighted in 2002 and awarded the Norton Medlicott Medal by the Historical Association in 2004. He was the historical adviser to three BBC series: *The Nazis: a Warning from History, War of the Century* and *Auschwitz*. His most recent books are *Hitler 1889–1936: Hubris* and *Hitler 1936–1945: Nemesis*, which received the Wolfson Literary Award for History and the Bruno Kreisky Prize in Austria for the Political Book of the Year, and was joint winner of the inaugural British Academy Book Prize; *Making Friends with Hitler: Lord Londonderry and Britain's Road to War*, which won the Elizabeth Longford Prize for Historical Biography in 2005; and *Fateful Choices: Ten Decisions that Changed the World, 1940–1941*. An abridged edition of *Hitler* was published in 2008.

Luck of the Devil is extracted from *Hitler 1936–1945: Nemesis*.

IAN KERSHAW

Luck of the Devil

The Story of Operation Valkyrie

PENGUIN BOOKS

PENGUIN BOOKS

Published by the Penguin Group
Penguin Books Ltd, 80 Strand, London WC2R ORL, England
Penguin Group (USA) Inc., 375 Hudson Street, New York, New York 10014, USA
Penguin Group (Canada), 90 Eglinton Avenue East, Suite 700, Toronto, Ontario, Canada M4P 2Y3
(a division of Pearson Penguin Canada Inc.)
Penguin Ireland, 25 St Stephen's Green, Dublin 2, Ireland
(a division of Penguin Books Ltd)
Penguin Group (Australia), 250 Camberwell Road, Camberwell, Victoria 3124, Australia
(a division of Pearson Australia Group Pty Ltd)
Penguin Books India Pvt Ltd, 11 Community Centre, Panchsheel Park, New Delhi – 110 017, India
Penguin Group (NZ), 67 Apollo Drive, Rosedale, North Shore 0632, New Zealand
(a division of Pearson New Zealand Ltd)
Penguin Books (South Africa) (Pty) Ltd, 24 Sturdee Avenue, Rosebank, Johannesburg 2196, South Africa

Penguin Books Ltd, Registered Offices: 80 Strand, London WC2R ORL, England

www.penguin.com

First published in *Hitler 1936–1945: Nemesis* by Allen Lane 2000
This adapted extract first published in Penguin Books 2009
1

Copyright © Ian Kershaw, 2000, 2009
All rights reserved

All documents (except document 4) are taken from *Germans Against Hitler, July 20, 1944*,
published by the Press and Information Office of the Federal Government of Germany.
Document 4 is from Bundesarchiv/Militararchiv, RH 12–21/8.

Set in 11/14 pt Linotype Sabon
Typeset by Rowland Phototypesetting Ltd, Bury St Edmunds, Suffolk
Printed in England by Clays Ltd, St Ives plc

978-0-141-04006-6

www.greenpenguin.co.uk

Penguin Books is committed to a sustainable future
for our business, our readers and our planet.
The book in your hands is made from paper
certified by the Forest Stewardship Council.

Mixed Sources
Product group from well-managed
forests and other controlled sources
www.fsc.org Cert no. SA-COC-1592
© 1996 Forest Stewardship Council
FSC

Contents

* All documents, except no. 4, are taken from *Germans Against Hitler, July 20, 1944*, published by the Press and Information Office of the Federal Government of Germany, fifth edition, 1969. In some places, the translation has been amended. The extracts in document no. 4 are drawn, respectively, from Bundesarchiv / Militärarchiv, RH 12-21/8, and Peter Hoffmann, 'Oberst i. G. Henning von Tresckow und die Staatsstreichpläne im Jahr 1943', *Vierteljahrshefte für Zeitgeschichte*, Heft 2, (2007), p. 358.

List of Illustrations

'It's not a matter any more of the practical aim, but of showing the world and history that the German resistance movement at risk of life has dared the decisive stroke. Everything else is a matter of indifference alongside that.'

Major-General Henning von Tresckow, June 1944

'It is now time that something was done. But the man who has the courage to do something must do it in the knowledge that he will go down in German history as a traitor. If he does not do it, however, he will be a traitor to his own conscience.'

Colonel Claus Schenk Graf von Stauffenberg,
July 1944

'A tiny clique of ambitious, unconscionable, and at the same time criminal, stupid officers has forged a plot to eliminate me and at the same time to eradicate with me practically the staff of the German armed forces' leadership.'   Adolf Hitler, 21 July 1944

Hitler's response to the military disasters of the early summer of 1944 was characteristic: he blamed others, and sacked his commanders. Whatever Hitler's capabilities as a military strategist had been, they had paid dividends only while Germany held the whip-hand and lightning offensives had been possible. Once – irrevocably after the failure of Operation 'Citadel', the last, short-lived major German offensive in the Soviet Union, in summer 1943 – a defensive strategy had become the only one available, Hitler's inadequacies as supreme German warlord were fully exposed. As the records of the military conferences with his advisers indicate, it was not that he was wholly devoid of tactical knowledge, despite his lack of formal training. Nor was it the case, as was sometimes adumbrated in post-war apologetics of German generals, that professionals who knew better were invariably forced into compliance with the lunatic orders of an amateur military bungler. As the verbatim notes of the conferences show, Hitler's tactics were frequently neither inherently absurd, nor did they usually stand in crass contradiction to the military advice he was receiving.

Even so: at points of crisis, the tensions and conflicts invariably surfaced. And by 1944, the individual military crises were accumulating into one almighty, life-or-death crisis for the regime itself. Hitler's political adroitness was by this time long gone. He dismissed out of hand all contemplation of a possible attempt to reach a political solution. Bridges had been burnt (as he had indicated on several occasions); there was no way back. And, since he refused any notion of negotiating from a position other than one of strength, from which all his earlier successes had derived, there was in any case no opportunity to seek a peace settlement. The gambling instinct which had stood Hitler in such good stead down to 1941 had long since lost its effectiveness in what had become a backs-to-the-wall struggle. But the worse the situation became, the more disastrously self-destructive became Hitler's other overriding and irrational instinct – that 'will' alone would triumph over all adversity, even grossly disparate levels of manpower and weaponry. He was wont, on occasion, to compare – absurdly – the adversity he had often faced in his rise to power with the current adversity in the throes of a world war. In a sense, his own invariable resort – all the more, the worse the crisis became – to a simple belief in 'triumph of the will' as the way out was indeed a replication of his attitude at critical junctures during the 'time of struggle' (such as the crisis of July 1921, which saw Hitler become party leader, or the crisis in December 1932, when the Party seemed on the verge of splitting). The innate self-destructive tendency which had been implicit in his all-or-nothing stance at such times now conveyed itself, catastrophically, to military leadership.

It was inevitable that seasoned military strategists and battle-hardened generals, schooled in more subtle forms of tactical command, would clash with him – often stridently – when their reading of the options available was so diametrically at variance with those of their supreme commander, and where the orders he emitted seemed to them so plainly militarily suicidal. They were also, however, schooled in obedience to orders of a superior; and Hitler was head of state, head of the armed forces, and since 1941 – disastrously – commander-in-chief (responsible for tactical decisions) of the army. Refusal to obey was not only an act of military insubordination; it was a treasonable act of political resistance.

Few were prepared to go down that route. But loyalty even to the extent of belief in the Führer's mission was no safeguard against dismissal if near-impossible demands were not met. In accordance with his warped logic, where 'will' had not triumphed, however fraught the circumstances, Hitler blamed the weakness or inadequacy of the commander. Another commander with a superior attitude, he presumed, would bring a different result – however objectively unfavourable the actual position. The commander of Army Group Centre, Field-Marshal Busch, a Hitler loyalist, correspondingly paid the price for the 'failure' of Army Group Centre during the onset of the massive Soviet offensive, 'Operation *Bagration*', that had been launched on 22 June 1944. He was dismissed by Hitler on 28 June, and replaced by one of his favourite commanders, the tough and energetic newly-promoted Field-Marshal Walter Model (who at the same time retained his command of Army Group North Ukraine) – dubbed by some, given the frequency with which he was charged with tackling a crisis, 'Hitler's fireman'.

Within days, there was a change of command, too, in the west. Reports to the Supreme Command of the Wehrmacht submitted by the Commander-in-Chief, Field-Marshal von Rundstedt, and the Commander of Panzer Group West, General Geyr von Schweppenburg, had drawn a pessimistic picture of the prospects of holding the lines against enemy inroads in France following the D-Day landings. General Alfred Jodl, chief of the Wehrmacht Operations Staff, played to Hitler's sentiments by noting that this meant the first step towards the evacuation of France following the D-Day landings. The report had followed similarly realistic assessments of the situation on the western front delivered by Rundstedt and Field-Marshal Erwin Rommel at the Berghof, Hitler's alpine retreat near Berchtesgaden, two days earlier, on 29 June. On 3 July, Rundstedt received a handwritten notice of his dismissal from Hitler. Officially, he had been replaced on grounds of health. The sacking of Geyr and Field-Marshal Hugo Sperrle, who had been responsible for air-defences in the West, also followed. Rundstedt's replacement, Field-Marshal Günther von Kluge, at that time high in Hitler's esteem, arrived in France, as General Heinz Guderian later put it, 'still filled with the optimism that prevailed at Supreme Headquarters'. He soon learnt differently.

Another military leader who fell irredeemably from grace at this time was Chief of the General Staff Kurt

Zeitzler. When appointed as replacement to Franz Halder in September 1942, Zeitzler had impressed Hitler with his drive, energy, and fighting spirit – the type of military leader he wanted. The relationship had palled visibly since the spring of 1944, when Hitler had pinned a major part of the blame for the loss of the Crimea on Zeitzler. By May, Zeitzler was indicating his wish to resign. The Chief of Staff's strong backing at the end of June for withdrawing the threatened Army Group North in the Baltic to a more defensible line, and his pessimism about the situation on the western front, amounted to the last straw. Zeitzler could no longer see the rationale of Hitler's tactics; Hitler was contemptuous of what he saw as the defeatism of Zeitzler and the General Staff. At the end of his tether following furious rows with Hitler, Zeitzler simply disappeared from the Berghof on 1 July. He had suffered a nervous breakdown. Hitler never spoke to him again. He would have Zeitzler dismissed from the Wehrmacht in January 1945, refusing him the right to wear uniform. Until his replacement, Guderian, was appointed on 21 July, the army was effectively without a Chief of the General Staff.

The Soviet advance had left the Red Army, in the northern sector of the front, poised not far from Vilna in Lithuania. Already, the borders of East Prussia were in their sights. On 9 July, Hitler left the Bavarian mountains and flew with Field-Marshal Wilhelm Keitel (head of the Wehrmacht High Command), Grand Admiral Karl Dönitz, Reichsführer SS Heinrich Himmler, and Luftwaffe Chief of Staff General Günther Korten back to his old headquarters near Rastenburg in East Prussia.

Field-Marshal Model and General Johannes Frießner, recently appointed as commander of Army Group North in place of General Georg Lindemann, joined them from the eastern front. The discussions ranged mainly over plans for the urgent creation of a number of new divisions to shore up the eastern front and protect any inroads into East Prussia. Model and Frießner sounded optimistic. Hitler, too, thought his Luftwaffe adjutant, Captain Nicolaus von Below, also remained positive about developments on the eastern front. Hitler flew back to the Berghof that afternoon. He had already hinted that, in the light of the situation in the east, he would have to move his headquarters back to East Prussia, even though the fortifications of his accommodation there were still incomplete. Reading between the lines of one or two comments, Below gained the impression, he later wrote, that during what were to prove Hitler's last days at the Berghof, before he left on 14 July for the Wolf's Lair, never to return, he was no longer under any illusions about the outcome of the war. Even so, any hints of pessimism were more than countered by repeated stress on continuing the war, the impact of the new weapons, and ultimate victory. Once more, it was plain to Below that Hitler would never capitulate. There would be no repeat of 1918. Hitler's political 'mission' had been based from the outset on that premise. The entire Reich would go down in flames first.

Hitler had lived amid the relative tranquillity of the Obersalzberg for almost four months. The regular entourage at the Berghof had dwindled somewhat in that time. And in the days before departure there had been few guests to enliven proceedings. Hitler himself had seemingly become more reserved. On the last evening, perhaps sensing he would not see the Berghof again, he had paused in front of the pictures hanging in the great hall. Then he had kissed the hand of Below's wife and Frau Brandt, the wife of one of his doctors, bidding them farewell. Next morning, 14 July, he flew back to East Prussia, returning to a Wolf's Lair now heavily re-inforced and scarcely recognizable from its appearance when first set up in 1941. He arrived in the late morning. At one o'clock he was running the military conference there as if he had never been away. He was more stooping in his gait than earlier. But his continued strength of will, despite the massive setbacks, continued to impress the admiring Below. For others, this strength of will – or obstinate refusal to face reality – was precisely what was preventing an end to the war and dragging Germany to inevitable catastrophe. They were determined to act before it was too late – to save what was left of the Reich, lay the foundations of a future without Hitler, and show the outside world that there was 'another Germany' beyond the forces of Nazism.

Among the conferences held during the last days at the Berghof were two, on 6 and 11 July, related to the mobilization of the 'home army' (*Heimatheer*). They were attended by a young officer with a patch over one eye, a shortened right arm, and two fingers missing from his left hand – all the consequence of serious injuries suffered during the African campaign. The officer, Colonel Claus Schenk Graf von Stauffenberg, chief of staff since 1 July to Colonel-General Friedrich Fromm,

Commander-in-Chief of the reserve army, was present, a day after Hitler's arrival at the Wolf's Lair, at a further conference about strengthening the home army.

The question of creating new divisions from the home army was once more on the agenda for the military conference on 20 July. Again, Stauffenberg was ordered to be present.

This time, he planted a time-bomb, carried in his briefcase, under the oaken table in the centre of the wooden barracks where Hitler was holding the conference. Hitler began the briefing, half an hour earlier than usual, at 12.30p.m. Fifteen minutes later the bomb exploded.

*   *   *

Stauffenberg's attempt to kill Hitler on 20 July 1944 had a lengthy prehistory. The complex strands of this prehistory contained in no small measure profound manifestations and admixtures of high ethical values and a transcendental sense of moral duty, codes of honour, political idealism, religious convictions, personal courage, remarkable selflessness, deep humanity, and a love of country that was light-years removed from Nazi chauvinism. The prehistory was also replete – how could it have been otherwise in the circumstances? – with disagreements, doubts, mistakes, miscalculations, moral dilemmas, short-sightedness, hesitancy, ideological splits, personal clashes, bungling organization, distrust – and sheer bad luck.

The origins of a *coup d'état* to eliminate Hitler dated back to the Sudeten crisis of 1938. Hitler's determination to risk war with the western powers and court disaster for Germany had at that time prompted a number of highly placed figures in the Army High Command, diplomatic service, and the Abwehr (the intelligence service), together with a circle of their close contacts, to plot to remove him should he attack Czechoslovakia. Though fraught with difficulties, the conspiracy had, in fact, taken shape by the time that Chamberlain's readiness to come to terms with Hitler at Bad Godesberg, then at Munich, removed the opportunity and took the wind out of the sails of the plotters. Their planned action might, in any case, have failed to materialize. The following summer, as the threat of war loomed ever larger, the same band of individuals had attempted to revive the conspiracy that had faltered with the Munich Agreement. But the fainter flickerings of opposition a year after Munich had come to nothing – floundering on internal divisions, Hitler's continued popularity among the masses, and, not least, the loyalty (if at times appearing to waver – reluctant, but ultimately and decisively intact) of the army chiefs whose support for any coup was vital. The same ingredients would hamper the conspiracy against Hitler in immensely more difficult conditions during the war itself.

A Swabian joiner, Georg Elser, had, working alone, shared none of the hesitancy of those operating from within the power-echelons of the regime. He had acted incisively with his bomb planted in the Bürgerbräukeller on the night of 8 November 1939, and come within a whisker of sending Hitler into oblivion. Good fortune alone had saved Hitler on that occasion: the bomb had exploded when he was on his way back to Berlin after delivering a much shorter address than usual to the Party's 'Old Guard', assembled on the traditional commemoration of the failed 1923 putsch. But outside the actions of a lone assassin, with the left-wing underground resistance groups, though never eliminated, weak, isolated, and devoid of access to the corridors of power, the only hope of toppling Hitler thereafter lay with those who themselves occupied positions of some power or influence in the regime itself.

On the fringes of the conspiracy, the participation in Nazi rule in itself naturally created ambivalence. Breaking oaths of loyalty was no light matter, even for some whose dislike of Hitler was evident. Prussian values were here a double-edged sword: a deep sense of obedience to authority and service to the state clashed with equally profound feelings of duty to God and to country. Whichever triumphed within an individual: whether heavy-hearted acceptance of service to a head of state regarded as legitimately constituted, however detested; or rejection of such allegiance in the interest of what was taken to be the greater good, should the head of state be leading the country to ruin; this was a matter for conscience and judgement. It could, and did, go either way.

Though there were numerous exceptions to a broad generalization, generational differences played some part. The tendency was greater in a younger generation of officers, for example, than in those who had already attained the highest ranks of general or field-marshal, to entertain thoughts of active participation in an attempt to overthrow the head of state. This was implied in a remark by Stauffenberg himself, several months before his attempt on Hitler's life: 'Since the generals have so far managed nothing, the colonels have now to step in.' On the other hand, views on the morality of assassinating the head of state – in the midst of an external struggle of titanic proportions against an enemy whose victory threatened the very existence of a German state – differed fundamentally on moral, not simply generational, grounds. Any attack on the head of state constituted, of course, high treason. But in a war, distinguishing this from treachery against one's own country, from betrayal to the enemy, was chiefly a matter of individual persuasion and the relative weighting of moral values. And only a very few were in a position to accumulate detailed and first-hand experiences of gross inhumanity at the same time as possessing the means to bring about Hitler's removal. Even fewer were prepared to act.

Beyond ethical considerations, there was the existential fear of the awesome consequences – for the families as well as for the individuals themselves – of discovery of any complicity in a plot to remove the head of state and instigate a *coup d'état*. This was certainly enough to deter many who were sympathetic to the aims of the plotters but unwilling to become involved. Nor was it just the constant dangers of discovery and physical risks that acted as a deterrent. There was also the isolation of resistance. To enter into, even to flirt with, the conspiracy against Hitler meant acknowledging an inner distance from friends, colleagues, comrades, entry into a twilight world of immense peril, and of social, ideological, even moral isolation.

Quite apart from the evident necessity, in a terroristic police state, of minimizing risks through maximum secrecy, the conspirators were themselves well aware of their lack of popular support. Even at this juncture, as the military disasters mounted and ultimate catastrophe beckoned, the fanatical backing for Hitler had by no means evaporated and continued, if as a minority taste, to show remarkable resilience and strength. Those still bound up with the dying regime, those who had invested in it, had committed themselves to it, had burnt their boats with it, were still true believers in the Führer, were likely to stop at nothing, as adversity mounted, in their unbridled retribution for any sign of opposition. But beyond the fanatics, there were many others who – naïvely, or after deep reflection – thought it not merely wrong, but despicable and treacherous, to undermine one's own country in war. Stauffenberg summed up the conspirators' dilemma a few days before he laid the bomb in the Wolf's Lair: 'It is now time that something was done. But the man who has the courage to do some-thing must do it in the knowledge that he will go down in German history as a traitor. If he does not do it, however, he will be a traitor to his own conscience.'

As this implies, the need to avoid a stab-in-the-back legend such as that which had followed the end of the First World War and left such a baleful legacy for the ill-fated Weimar Republic was a constant burden and anxiety for those who had decided – sometimes with a heavy heart – that Germany's future rested on their capacity to remove Hitler, violently or not, from the scene, constitute a new government, and seek peace terms. This was one important reason why, from 1938 onwards, the leading figures in the resistance fatefully awaited the 'right moment' – which never came. Fearful of cutting down a national hero who had just won scarcely imaginable triumphs (which, in some cases, they themselves had cheered, and were captivated by) they felt incapacitated as long as Hitler was chalking up one apparent success after another before the war, then in the wave of blitzkrieg victories. But, also worried about the consequences of removing Hitler and seeming to stab the war effort in the back after a major disaster, the hesitancy continued when final victory had become no more than a chimera. Rather than controlling the moment for a strike, the conspirators let it rest on external contingencies that, in the nature of things, they could not orchestrate.

When the strike eventually came, with the invasion consolidated in the west and the Red Army pressing towards the borders of the Reich in the east, the conspirators themselves recognized that they had missed the chance to influence the possible outcome of the war through their action. As one of their key driving-forces, Major-General Henning von Tresckow, from late 1943 chief of staff of the 2nd Army in the southern section of the eastern front, put it: 'It's not a matter any more of the practical aim, but of showing the world and history that the German resistance movement at risk of life has dared the decisive stroke (*Wurf*). Everything else is a matter of indifference alongside that.'

*   *   *

All prospects of opposition to Hitler had been dimmed following the astonishing chain of military successes between autumn 1939 and spring 1941. Then, following the promulgation of the notorious Commissar Law, ordering the liquidation of captured Red Army political commissars, it had been Colonel (as he was at the time) Henning von Tresckow, Field-Marshal Fedor von Bock's first general staff officer at Army Group Centre, who had been instrumental in revitalizing thoughts of resistance among a number of front officers – some of them purposely selected on account of their anti-regime stance. Born in 1901, tall, balding, with a serious demeanour, a professional soldier, fervent upholder of Prussian values, cool and reserved but at the same time a striking and forceful personality, disarmingly modest, but with iron determination, Tresckow had been an early admirer of Hitler though he had soon turned into an unbending critic of the lawless and inhumane policies of the regime. Those whom Tresckow was able to bring to Army Group Centre included close allies in the emerging conspiracy against Hitler, notably Fabian von Schlabrendorff – six years younger than Tresckow himself, trained in law, who would serve as a liaison between Army Group Centre and other focal points of the conspiracy – and Rudolph-Christoph Freiherr von Gersdorff, born in 1905, a professional soldier, already an arch-critic of Hitler, and now located in a key position in the intelligence section of Army Group Centre. But attempts to persuade Bock, together with the other two group commanders on the eastern front, Rundstedt and Field-Marshal Wilhelm Ritter von Leeb, to confront Hitler and refuse orders failed. Any realistic prospect of opposition from the front disappeared again until late 1942. By then, in the wake of the unfolding Stalingrad crisis and seeing Hitler as responsible for the certain ruin of Germany, Tresckow was ready to assassinate him.

During the course of 1942, a number of focal points of practically dormant opposition within Germany itself – army and civilian – had begun to flicker back to life. The savagery of the warfare on the eastern front and, in the light of the winter crisis of 1941–2, the magnitude of the calamity towards which Hitler was steering Germany, had revitalized the notion, still less than concrete, that something must be done. Ludwig Beck (former Chief of the Army General Staff), Carl Goerdeler (one-time Price Commissar), Johannes Popitz (Prussian Finance Minister), and Ulrich Hassell (earlier the German Ambassador in Rome) – all connected with the pre-war conspiracy that had come to nothing at the time of the Munich Agreement in 1938 – met up again in Berlin in March 1942, but decided there were as yet few prospects. Even so, it was agreed that former Chief of Staff Beck would serve as a central point for the embryonic opposition. Meetings were held soon after with Colonel Hans Oster – head of the central office dealing with foreign intelligence in the Abwehr, the driving-force behind the 1938 conspiracy, who had leaked Germany's invasion plans to Holland in 1940 – and Hans von Dohnanyi, a jurist who had also played a significant part in the 1938 plot, and, like Oster, used his position in the foreign section of the Abwehr to develop good contacts to officers with oppositional tendencies. Around the same time, Oster engineered a close link to a new and important recruit to the oppositional groups, General Friedrich Olbricht, head of the General Army Office in Berlin and Fromm's deputy as commander of the home army. Olbricht, born in 1888 and a career soldier, was not one to seek the limelight. He epitomized the desk-general, the organizer, the military administrator. But he was unusual in his pro-Weimar attitude before 1933, and, thereafter – driven largely by Christian and patriotic feelings – in his consistent anti-Hitler stance, even amid the jubilation of the foreign-policy triumphs of the 1930s and the victories of the first phase of the war. His role would emerge as the planner of the *coup d'état* that was to follow upon the successful assassination of Hitler.

Already as the Stalingrad crisis deepened towards the end of 1942, Tresckow – later described by the Gestapo as 'without doubt one of the driving-forces and the "evil spirit" of the putschist circles', and allegedly referred to by Stauffenberg as his 'guiding master' (*Lehrmeister*) – was pressing for the assassination of Hitler without delay. He had become convinced that nothing could be expected of the top military leadership in initiating a coup. 'They would only follow an order,' was his view. He took it upon himself to provide the 'ignition (*Initialzündung*)', as the conspirators labelled the assassination of Hitler that would lead to their removal of the Nazi leadership and takeover of the state. Tresckow had already in the summer of 1942 commissioned Gersdorff with the task of obtaining suitable explosives. The latter acquired and tested various devices, including British explosives intended for sabotage and for the

French Resistance that had been captured following an ill-fated commando expedition to St Nazaire and a catastrophic assault on Dieppe in 1942. Eventually, he and Tresckow settled on a small British magnetic device, a 'clam' (or type of adhesive mine) about the size of a book, ideal for sabotage and easy to conceal. Olbricht, meanwhile, coordinated the links with the other conspirators in Berlin and laid the groundwork for a coup to take place in March. The plans to occupy important civilian and military positions in Berlin and other major cities were, in essence, along the lines that were to be followed in July 1944.

One obvious problem was how to get close enough to Hitler to carry out an assassination. Hitler's movements were unpredictable. He frequently – not just for security reasons – altered his plans at the last minute. Such an undependable schedule had in mid-February 1943 vitiated the intention of two officers, General Hubert Lanz and Major-General Hans Speidel, of arresting Hitler on an expected visit to Army Group B headquarters at Poltava. The visit did not materialize. When Hitler suddenly decided to visit the front, on 17 February, it had been to Zaporozhye not Poltava (which Army Group B had in any case by then left). Hitler's personal security had, meanwhile, been tightened considerably. He was invariably surrounded by SS bodyguards, pistols at the ready, and was always driven by his own chauffeur, Erich Kempka, in one of his own limousines which were stationed at different points in the Reich and in the occupied territories. And Major-General Rudolf Schmundt, Hitler's Wehrmacht adjutant, had told Tresckow and Gersdorff that Hitler wore a bullet-proof vest and hat. This helped persuade them that the possibilities of a selected assassin having time to pull out his pistol, aim accurately, and ensure that his shot would kill Hitler were not great. Nor was the chosen sharp-shooter, bearer of the Iron Cross with Oak Leaves Lieu-tenant-Colonel Georg Freiherr von Boeselager, sure that he was mentally equipped to shoot down a person – even Hitler – in cold blood. It was an entirely different proposition, he felt, from firing at an anonymous enemy in war.

Nevertheless, Boeselager made preparations for a group of officers, who had declared themselves ready to do so, to shoot Hitler on a visit which, it was hoped, he would soon pay to Army Group Centre headquarters at Smolensk. The visit eventually took place on 13 March. The plan to shoot him in the mess of Field-Marshal von Kluge, commander of Army Group Centre, was abandoned since there was a distinct possibility of Kluge and other senior officers being killed alongside Hitler. Given Kluge's wavering and two-faced attitude towards the conspiracy against Hitler, more cynical plotters might have thought the risk well worthwhile. As it was, they took the view that the loss of Kluge and other leading personnel from Army Group Centre would ser-iously weaken still further the shaky eastern front. The idea shifted to shooting Hitler as he walked the short distance back to his car from headquarters. But having infiltrated the security cordon around him and set up position to open fire, the assassination squad failed to carry out their plan. Whether this was because Hitler took a different route back to his car, or whether – the more likely explanation – the danger of killing Kluge and other officers from the Group was seen as too great, is unclear.

Tresckow reverted to the original plan to blow up Hitler. During the meal at which, had the original plans been carried out, Hitler would have been shot, Tresckow asked one of the Führer's entourage, Lieutenant-Colonel Heinz Brandt, travelling in Hitler's plane, to take back a package for him to Colonel Hellmuth Stieff in Army High Command. This was in itself nothing unusual. Packages were often sent to and from the front by personal delivery when transport happened to be available. Tresckow said it was part of a bet with Stieff. The package looked like two bottles of cognac. It was, in fact, two parts of the British clam-bomb that Tresckow had put together.

Schlabrendorff carried the package to the aerodrome and gave it to Brandt just as he was climbing into Hitler's Condor ready for take-off. Moments before, Schlabrendorff had pressed the fuse capsule to activate the detonator, set for thirty minutes. It could be expected that Hitler would be blown from the skies shortly before the plane reached Minsk. Schlabrendorff returned as quickly as possible to headquarters and informed the Berlin opposition in the Abwehr that the 'ignition' for the coup had been undertaken. But no news came of an explosion. The tension among Tresckow's group was palpable. Hours later, they heard that Hitler had landed safely at Rastenburg. Schlabrendorff gave the code-word through to Berlin that the attempt had failed. Why there had been no explosion was a mystery. Probably the intense cold had prevented the detonation. For the nervous conspirators, ruminations about the likely cause of failure now took second place to the vital need to recover the incriminating package. Tresckow rang up Brandt to say a mistake had occurred, and he should hold on to the package. Next morning, Schlabrendorff flew to Army High Command with two genuine bottles of cognac, retrieved the bomb, retreated to privacy, cautiously opened the packet with a razor-blade, and with great relief defused it. Mixed with relief, the disappointment among the opposition at such a lost chance was intense.

Immediately, however, another opportunity beckoned. Gersdorff had the possibility of attending the 'Heroes' Memorial Day', to take place on 21 March 1943 in Berlin. Gersdorff declared himself ready to sacrifice his own life in order to blow up Hitler during the ceremony. Tresckow, for his part, assured Gersdorff that the coup to follow Hitler's assassination would lead to an agreement with the western powers for capitulation while continuing the defence of the Reich in the east and introducing a democratic form of government. With some difficulty, problems of ensuring that Gersdorff would be close enough to Hitler to bring off the assassination, and problems of establishing precisely what time the ceremonials would begin – given security precautions, betrayal of this fact was in itself dubbed sufficient to warrant the death penalty – were overcome. The timing of the attempt was a third problem. The best fuse that Gersdorff could come up with lasted ten minutes. The ceremony itself, in the glass-covered courtyard of the Zeughaus, the old arsenal, on Unter den Linden, the beautiful tree-lined boulevard running through the centre of Berlin, presented no possibility of detonating an explosion in his close proximity. And once Hitler was outside, inspecting the guard of honour at the war memorial on Unter den Linden, laying the wreath, speaking to selected wounded soldiers, or conversing with guests of honour, Gersdorff would have no cause to be near him. His chance would have gone.

The attempt had to be made, therefore, while Hitler was visiting the exhibition of captured Soviet war booty, laid on to fill in the time between the ceremony in the Zeughaus and the wreath-laying at the cenotaph. Gersdorff positioned himself at the entry to the exhibition, in the rooms of the Zeughaus. He raised his right arm to greet Hitler as the dictator came by. At the same moment, with his left hand, he pressed the detonator charge on the bomb. He expected Hitler to be in the exhibition for half an hour, more than enough time for the bomb to go off. But this year, Hitler raced through the exhibition, scarcely glancing at the material assembled for him, and was outside within two minutes. Gersdorff could follow Hitler no further. He sought out the nearest toilet and deftly defused the bomb.

Once again, astonishing luck had accompanied Hitler. Whether it was concern about the possibility of an allied air-raid or whether Hitler's security advisers had given a hint of concern for his safety at a public appearance, given the uneasy atmosphere after Stalingrad, when, following the 'White Rose' protests of the Munich students Hans and Sophie Scholl and their friends (arrested and swiftly executed after distributing leaflets attacking Hitler), rumours of an attempt to overthrow the regime were circulating; or whether Hitler himself, ill-attuned to having to give a public performance in sensitive circumstances while the country was reeling from such a military disaster, had scant feeling for the ceremonials and simply wanted to get them over with: whatever the reason, yet another attempt, conscientiously planned despite the difficulties, and undertaken at notable risk, had failed. A new opportunity would not rapidly present itself.

The depressed and shocked mood following Stalingrad had probably also offered the best possible psychological moment for a coup against Hitler. A successful undertaking at that time might, despite the recently announced 'Unconditional Surrender' strategy of the Allies, have stood a chance of splitting them. The removal of the Nazi leadership and offer of capitulation in the west that Tresckow intended would at any rate have placed the western Allies in a quandary about whether to respond to peace-feelers.

Overtures by opposition groups to the western Allies had been systematically rebuffed long before this time. For example, for his pains in liaising with German churchmen belonging to the resistance who wanted to sound out the British government about their attitude towards a Germany without Hitler, Bishop George Bell of Chichester was described by Anthony Eden, the British Foreign Secretary, in words redolent of those once allegedly used by King Henry II to usher in the murder of Archbishop Thomas Becket in 1170, as a 'pestilent priest'. Despite long-standing contacts with leading figures in the conspiracy – including Carl Goerdeler, the diplomat Adam von Trott, and the radically-minded evangelical pastor Dietrich Bonhoeffer (who had spent some time in ministry at the German church in south London) – the resistance was regarded by the British war leadership (and the Americans shared the view) as little more than a hindrance. A successful coup from within could, it was felt, endanger the alliance with the Soviet Union – exactly the strategy which the conspirators were hoping to achieve – and would cause difficulties in establishing the post-war order in Germany. The key criterion was how far action by those within Germany who opposed Hitler would contribute to the Allied war effort. A British government internal memorandum written little over a month before Stauffenberg's bomb went off in Hitler's headquarters gave a clear answer: 'There is no initiative we can take vis-à-vis "dissident" German groups or individuals, military or civilian, which holds out the smallest prospect of affording practical assistance to our present military operations in the West.'

Though prepared to distinguish between the Nazi leadership and the German people, Allied thinking was less ready to separate Hitler and his henchmen from his military leaders and from the Prussian traditions which, it was thought, had been a major cause of two world wars. Now, with the war turning remorselessly in their favour, the Allies were less than ever inclined to give much truck to an internal opposition which, it appeared, had claimed much but achieved nothing, and, furthermore, entertained expectations of holding on to some of the territorial gains that Hitler had made.

This was indeed the case, certainly with some of the older members of the national-conservative group aligned to Goerdeler whose break with Hitler had already taken place in the mid-1930s. Goerdeler and those loosely connected with him – notably Beck, Hassell, Popitz, and ex-Nazi enthusiast and Berlin professor of politics and economics Jens Jessen – despised the barbarism of the Nazi regime. But they were keen to re-establish Germany's status as a major power, and continued to see the Reich dominating central and eastern Europe. Goerdeler, presumed to be the new Reich Chancellor in a post-Hitlerian government, had envisaged in early 1942 'a European federation of states under German leadership within 10 or 20 years' if the war could be ended and a 'sensible political system' put in place. In summer 1943, despite the drastic deterioration of Germany's military situation, Goerdeler's incorrigible optimism still led him to put forward as his foreign-political aims: the restoration of the eastern borders of 1914 (meaning, of course, keeping the Polish Corridor, reacquired by Germany through immeasurable barbarism); retention of Austria and the Sudetenland, along with Eupen-Malmedy and the South Tyrol (which even Hitler had not annexed); negotiations with France over Alsace-Lorraine; undiminished German sovereignty; no reparations; and economic union in Europe (outside Russia).

As regards the nature of a post-Nazi regime, the notions of the national conservatives, disdaining the plebiscitary and demagogic characteristics of what they saw as populist mass politics, were essentially (despite differences of emphasis) oligarchic and authoritarian. They favoured a restoration of the monarchy and limited electoral rights in self-governing communities, resting on Christian family values – the embodiment of the true 'national community' which the Nazis had corrupted.

Among the most striking features of Goerdeler's lack of realism was his conviction, when it was put to him that Hitler would have to be forcefully removed from the scene, that he could be persuaded by reasoned argument to step down. His expectation of an unbloody coup even led him to the idea of suggesting that he could eliminate Hitler through open debate if the military could provide him with the opportunity to address the Wehrmacht and the people. It was as well that a letter, which he composed in May 1944, containing such a remarkable suggestion was sent back by Stieff and never passed to Chief of Staff Zeitzler.

The notions of Goerdeler and his close associates, whose age, mentality, and upbringing inclined them to look back to the pre-1914 Reich for much of their inspiration, found little favour among a group of a younger generation (mainly born during the first decade of the twentieth century) which gained its common identity through outright opposition to Hitler and his regime. The group, whose leaders were mainly of aristocratic descent, came to be known as 'the Kreisau Circle', a term coined by the Gestapo and drawn from the estate in Silesia where the group held a number of its meetings. The estate belonged to one of its central figures, Helmuth James Graf von Moltke, born in 1907, trained in law, a great admirer of British traditions, a descendant of the famous Chief of the General Staff of the Prussian army in Bismarck's era. The ideas of the 'Kreisau Circle' for a 'new order' after Hitler dated back in embryo to 1940, when they were first elaborated by Moltke and his close friend and relative Peter Graf Yorck von Wartenburg, three years older, also trained in law, a formative figure in the group, and with good contacts to the military opposition. Both had rejected Nazism and its gross inhumanity from an early stage. By 1942–3 they were drawing to meetings at Kreisau and in Berlin a number of like-minded friends and associates, ranging across social classes and denominational divisions, including the former Oxford Rhodes Scholar and foreign-policy spokesman of the group Adam von Trott zu Solz, the Social Democrat Carlo Mierendorff, the socialist pedagogical expert Adolf Reichwein, the Jesuit priest Pater Alfred Delp, and the Protestant pastor Eugen Gerstenmaier.

Unlike the Goerdeler group, the 'Kreisau Circle' drew heavily for its inspiration on the idealism of the German youth movement, socialist and Christian philosophies, and experiences of the post-war misery and rise of National Socialism. Moltke, Yorck, and their associates – unlike the Goerdeler group – had no desire to hold on to expectations of German hegemony on the continent. They looked instead to a future in which national sovereignty (and the nationalist ideologies which underpinned it) would give way to a federal Europe, modelled in part on the United States of America. They were well aware that major territorial concessions would have to be made by Germany, along with some form of reparation for the peoples of Europe who had suffered so grievously under Nazi rule. They saw an international tribunal to deal with war criminals as a basis for weaning the German people from its attachment to National Socialism. And they looked to a strong international organization to preserve equal rights for all countries of the world. Their concept of a new form of state rested heavily upon German Christian and social ideals, looking to democratization from below, through self-governing communities working on the basis of social justice, guaranteed by a central state that was little more than an umbrella organization for localized and particularized interests within a federal structure.

Such notions were inevitably utopian. The 'Kreisau Circle' had no arms to back it, and no access to Hitler. It was dependent upon the army for action. Moltke, who opposed assassination, and Yorck, quite especially, pressed on a number of occasions for a coup to unseat Hitler. By 1943, Moltke's distrust of the German military leadership on account of its complicity in so much of the Nazi barbarism led him to advocate American military support for a new oppositional German government. Allied troops were to be parachuted into German cities to back a coup.

Such an illusory hope still left out of the equation the initial step: how to remove Hitler, and who should do it. This, rather than utopian visions of a future social and political order, was the primary issue that continued to preoccupy Tresckow and his fellow officers who had committed themselves to the opposition. The problem became, if anything, more rather than less difficult during the summer and autumn of 1943. Any expectation that Lieutenant-General Erich von Manstein might commit himself to the opposition was wholly dashed in the summer. 'Prussian field-marshals do not mutiny,' was his lapidary response to Gersdorff's probings. Manstein was at least honest and straightforward. Kluge, by contrast, blew hot and cold – offering backing to Tresckow and Gersdorff, then retreating from it. There was nothing to be gained from that quarter, though those in the opposition continued to persist in the delusion that Kluge was ultimately on their side.

There were other setbacks. Beck was meanwhile quite seriously ill. And Fritz-Dietlof Graf von der Schulenburg – a lawyer by training, who, after initially sympathizing with National Socialism and holding a number of high administrative positions in the regime, had come to serve as a liaison between the military and civilian opposition – was interrogated on suspicion that he was involved in plans for a coup, though later released. Others, including Dietrich Bonhoeffer, were also arrested, as the tentacles of the Gestapo threatened to entangle the leading figures in the resistance. Even worse: Hans von Dohnanyi and Hans Oster from the Abwehr were arrested in April, initially for alleged foreign currency irregularities, though this drew suspicion on their involvement in political opposition. The head of the Abwehr, Admiral Wilhelm Canaris, a professional obfuscater, managed for a time to throw sand in the eyes of the Gestapo agents. But as a centre of the resistance, the Abwehr had become untenable. By February 1944, its foreign department, which Oster had controlled, was incorporated into the Reich Security Head Office, and Canaris, dubious figure that he was for the opposition, himself placed under house arrest.

Tresckow, partly while on leave in Berlin, was tireless in attempting to drive on the plans for action against Hitler. But in October, he was stationed at the head of a regiment at the front, away from his previously influential position in Army Group Centre headquarters. At the same time, in any case, Kluge was injured in a car accident and replaced by Field-Marshal Ernst Busch, an outright Hitler loyalist, so that an assassination attempt from Army Group Centre could now be ruled out. At this point, Olbricht revived notions, previously enter-tained but never sustained, of carrying out both the strike against Hitler and the subsequent coup, not through the front army, but from the headquarters of the reserve army in Berlin. Finding an assassin with access to Hitler had been a major problem. Now, one was close at hand.

Claus Schenk Graf von Stauffenberg came from a Swabian aristocratic family. Born in 1907, the youngest of three brothers, he grew up under the influence of Catholicism – though his family were non-practising – and of the youth movement. He became particularly attracted to the ideas of the poet Stefan George, then held in extraordinary esteem by an impressionable circle of young admirers, strangely captivated by his vague, neo-conservative cultural mysticism which looked away from the sterilities of bourgeois existence towards a new élite of aristocratic aestheticism, godliness, and manliness. Like many young officers, Stauffenberg was initially attracted by aspects of National Socialism – not least its renewed emphasis on the value of strong armed forces and its anti-Versailles foreign policy – but rejected its racial antisemitism and, after the Blomberg–Fritsch crisis of early 1938 (when the War Minister and the Commander-in-Chief of the Army had been forced out of office in the wake of scandals in their private lives), was increasingly critical of Hitler and his drive to war. Even so, serving in Poland he was contemptuous of the Polish people, approved of the colonization of the country, and was enthusiastic about the German victory. He was still more jubilant after the stunning successes in the western campaign, and hinted that he had changed his views on Hitler.

The mounting barbarity of the regime nevertheless appalled him. And when he turned irredeemably against Hitler in the late spring of 1942, it was under the influence of incontrovertible eye-witness reports of massacres of Ukrainian Jews by SS men. Hearing the reports, Stauffenberg concluded that Hitler must be removed. As some of his critics pointed out, it was, compared with others, somewhat late in the day that he was finally persuaded to join the oppositional conspiracy. Serving in North Africa with the 10th Panzer Division, he was (as we noted) badly wounded in April 1943, losing his right eye, his right hand, and two fingers from his left hand. Soon after his discharge from hospital in August, speaking to Friedrich Olbricht about a new post as chief of staff in the General War Office (*Allgemeines Heeresamt*) in Berlin, he was tentatively asked about joining the resistance. There was little doubt what his answer would be. He had already come to the conclusion that the only way to deal with Hitler was to kill him.

By early September, Stauffenberg had been introduced to the leading figures in the opposition. So far as it can be deduced, his political stance, once he had come to join the resistance, had little or nothing in common with that of the national-conservatives – Goerdeler's views he treated almost with disdain – and was closer to that of the 'Kreisau Circle'. But, like Tresckow, Stauffenberg was a man of action, an organizer more than a theoretician. He deliberated with Tresckow in autumn 1943 about the best way to assassinate Hitler and the related but separate issue of organizing the coup to follow. As a means of taking over the state, they came up with the idea of recasting an operational plan, code-named 'Valkyrie', already devised by Olbricht and approved by Hitler, for mobilizing the reserve army within Germany in the event of serious internal unrest. The recouched plan began by denouncing, not anti-Nazi 'subversives', but putschists *within* the Nazi Party itself – 'an unscrupulous clique of non-combat Party leaders' which 'has tried to exploit the situation to stab the deeply committed front in the back, and to seize power for selfish purposes', demanding the proclamation of martial law. The aim of 'Valkyrie' had been to protect the regime; it was now transformed into a strategy for removing it.

Unleashing 'Valkyrie' posed two problems. The first was that the command had to be issued by the head of the reserve army. This was General Friedrich Fromm, born in 1888 into a Protestant family with strong military traditions, a huge man, somewhat reserved in character, with strong beliefs in the army as the guarantor of Germany's status as a world-power. Fromm was no outright Hitler loyalist, but a fence-sitter who remained non-committal in his cautious desire to keep his options open and back whichever came out on top, the regime or the putschists – a policy which would eventually backfire upon him. The other problem was the old one of access to Hitler. Tresckow had concluded that only an assassination attempt in Führer Headquarters could get round the unpredictability of Hitler's schedule and the tight security precautions surrounding him. The difficulty was to find someone prepared to carry out the attempt who had reason to be in Hitler's close proximity in Führer Headquarters.

Stauffenberg, who had brought new dynamism to the sagging momentum of the opposition, wanted a strike against Hitler by mid-November. But who would carry it out? Colonel Stieff, approached by Stauffenberg in October 1943, declined. The attempt had to be postponed. Colonel Joachim Meichßner from the Wehrmacht operational staff (*Wehrmachtführungsstab*) was subsequently asked, in spring 1944, if he might undertake it. He, too, declined. In the interim, Stauffenberg had been introduced to Captain Axel Freiherr von dem Bussche, whose courage in action had won him the Iron Cross, First Class, among other decorations. Witnessing a mass shooting of thousands of Jews in the Ukraine in October 1942 had been a searing experience for Bussche, and opened him to any prospect of doing away with Hitler and his regime. Approached by Stauffenberg, he was prepared to sacrifice his own life by springing on

Hitler with a detonated grenade while the Führer was visiting a display of new uniforms.

Bad luck continued to dog the plans. One such uniform display, in December 1943, had to be cancelled when the train carrying the new uniforms was hit in an air-raid and the uniforms destroyed. Before Bussche could be brought back for another attempt, he was badly wounded on the eastern front in January 1944, losing a leg and dropping out of consideration for Stauffenberg's plans.

Lieutenant Ewald Heinrich von Kleist, son of the Prussian landowner and longstanding critic of Hitler Ewald von Kleist-Schmenzin, expressed himself willing to take over. Everything was set for Hitler's visit to a uniform display in mid-February. But the display was once again cancelled.

Yet another chance arose when Rittmeister Eberhard von Breitenbuch, aide-de-camp to Field-Marshal Busch (Kluge's successor as Commander-in-Chief of Army Group Centre) and already initiated in plans to eliminate Hitler, had the opportunity to accompany Busch to a military briefing at the Berghof on 11 March 1944. Breitenbuch was uncertain about an attempt with a bomb, but had declared himself ready to shoot Hitler in the head. His Browning pistol was in his trouser pocket, and ready to fire as soon as he came close to Hitler. But on this occasion, ADCs were not permitted in the briefing. Luck was still on Hitler's side.

Even Stauffenberg began to lose heart – especially once the western Allies had established a firm footing on the soil of France. The Gestapo by now had the scent of the opposition; a number of arrests of leading figures pointed to the intensifying danger. Would it not now be better to await the inevitable defeat? Would even a successful strike against Hitler be anything more than a largely empty gesture? Tresckow gave the answer: it was vital that the coup took place, that the outside world should see that there was a German resistance movement prepared at the cost of its members' lives to topple such an unholy regime.

A last opportunity presented itself. On 1 July 1944, now promoted to colonel, Stauffenberg was appointed Fromm's chief of staff – in effect, his deputy. It provided him with what had been hitherto lacking: access to Hitler at military briefings related to the home army. He no longer needed to look for someone to carry out the assassination. He could do it himself. That this was the only solution became more evident than ever when Stieff declined a second request from Stauffenberg to try to kill Hitler at the display of uniforms finally taking place at Klessheim Palace, near Salzburg, on 7 July.

The difficulty with Stauffenberg taking over the role of assassin was that he would be needed at the same time in Berlin to organize the coup from the headquarters of the reserve army. The double role meant that the chances of failure were thereby enhanced. It was far from ideal. But the risk had to be taken.

On 6 July, Stauffenberg was present, for the first time in his capacity as chief of staff to Fromm, at two hour-long briefings at the Berghof. He had explosives with him. But, it seems, an appropriate opportunity did not present itself. Whatever the reason, at any rate, he made no attempt on this occasion. Impatient to act, Stauffenberg resolved to try at his next visit to the Berghof, five days later. But the absence of Himmler, whom the conspirators wanted to eliminate along with Hitler, deterred him. Again, nothing happened. On 15 July, when he was once more at Führer Headquarters (now moved back to the Wolf's Lair in East Prussia), Stauffenberg was determined to act. Once more, nothing happened. Most probably, it seems, he had been unable to set the charge in time for the first of the three briefings that afternoon. While the second short briefing was taking place, he was telephoning Berlin to clarify whether he should in any case go through with the attempt in the absence of Himmler. And during the third briefing, he was himself directly involved in the presentation, which deprived him of all possibility of priming the bomb and carrying out the attack. This time, Olbricht even issued the 'Valkyrie' order. It had to be passed off as a practice alarm-drill. The error could not be repeated. Next time, the issue of the 'Valkyrie' order could not go out ahead of the assassination attempt. It would have to wait for Stauffenberg's confirmation that Hitler was dead. After the bungling of the opportunity on the 15th, the third time that he had taken such a high risk to no avail, Stauffenberg prepared for what he told his fellow conspirators, gathered at his home in Berlin's Wannsee district on the evening of 16 July, would be a last attempt. This would take place during his next visit to the Wolf's Lair, in the briefing scheduled for 20 July.

*　　*　　*

After a two-hour flight from Berlin, Stauffenberg and his adjutant, Lieutenant Werner von Haeften, landed at Rastenburg at 10.15 a.m. on 20 July. Stauffenberg was immediately driven the four miles to the Wolf's Lair. Haeften accompanied Major-General Stieff, who had flown in the same plane, to Army High Command, before returning later to Führer Headquarters. By 11.30 a.m. Stauffenberg was in a pre-briefing, directed by Keitel, that lasted three-quarters of an hour. Time was pressing since Hitler's briefing, owing to the arrival of Mussolini that afternoon, was to take place half an hour earlier than usual, at 12.30 p.m.

As soon as the meeting with Keitel was over, Stauffenberg asked where he could freshen up and change his shirt. It was a hot day, and an unremarkable request; but he needed to hurry. Haeften, carrying the briefcase containing the bomb, met him in the corridor. As soon as they were in the toilet, they began hastily to prepare to set the time-fuses in the two explosive devices they had brought with them, and to place the devices, each weighing around a kilogram, in Stauffenberg's briefcase. Stauffenberg set the first charge. The bomb could go off any time after a quarter of an hour, given the hot and stuffy conditions, and would explode within half an hour at most. Outside, Keitel was getting impatient. Just then, a telephone call came from General Erich Fellgiebel, head of communications at Wehrmacht High Command and commissioned, in the plot against Hitler, with the vital task of blocking communications to and from the Führer Headquarters following an assassination attempt. Keitel's adjutant, Major Ernst John von Freyend, took the call. Fellgiebel wanted to speak to Stauffenberg and requested him to call back. There was no time for that. Freyend sent Sergeant-Major Werner Vogel to tell Stauffenberg of Fellgiebel's message, and to hurry him along. Vogel found Stauffenberg and Haeften busy with some object. On being told to hurry, Stauffenberg brusquely replied that he was on his way. Freyend then shouted that he should come along at once. Vogel waited by the open door. Stauffenberg hastily closed his brief-case. There was no chance of setting the time-fuse for the second device he and Haeften had brought with them. Haeften stuffed this, along with sundry papers, in his own bag. It was a decisive moment. Had the second device, even without the charge being set, been placed in Stauffenberg's bag along with the first, it would have been detonated by the explosion, more than doubling the effect. Almost certainly, in such an event, no one would have survived.

The briefing, taking place as usual in the wooden barrack-hut inside the high fence of the closely guarded inner perimeter of the Wolf's Lair, had already begun when Stauffenberg was ushered in. Hitler, seated in the middle of the long side of the table nearest to the door, facing the windows, was listening to Major-General Adolf Heusinger, chief of operations at General Staff headquarters, describe the rapidly worsening position on the eastern front. Hitler absent-mindedly shook hands with Stauffenberg, when Keitel introduced him, and returned to Heusinger's report. Stauffenberg had requested a place as close as possible to the Führer. His hearing disability, together with the need to have his papers close to hand when he reported on the creation of a number of new divisions from the reserve army to help block the Soviet breakthrough into Poland and East Prussia, gave him a good excuse. Room was found for him on Hitler's right, towards the end of the table. Freyend, who had carried Stauffenberg's briefcase into the room, placed it under the table, against the outside of the solid right-hand table-leg.

No sooner had he arrived in the room, than Stauffenberg made an excuse to leave it. This attracted no special attention. There was much to-ing and fro-ing during the daily conferences. Attending to important telephone calls or temporarily being summoned away was a regular occurrence. Stauffenberg left his cap and belt behind to suggest that he would be returning. Once outside the room, he asked Freyend to arrange the connection for the call which he still had to make to General Fellgiebel. But as soon as Freyend returned to the briefing, Stauffenberg hung up and hurried back to the Wehrmacht adjutants' building, where he met Haeften and Fellgiebel. Lieutenant Ludolf Gerhard Sander, a communications officer in Fellgiebel's department, was also there. Stauffenberg's absence in the briefing had meanwhile been noted; he had been needed to provide a point of information during Heusinger's presentation. But there was no sinister thought in anyone's mind at this point. At the adjutancy, Stauffenberg and Haeften were anxiously making arrangements for the car that had been organized to rush them to the airfield. At that moment, they heard a deafening explosion from the direction of the barracks. Fellgiebel gave Stauffenberg

a startled look. Stauffenberg shrugged his shoulders.
Sander seemed unsurprised. Mines around the complex
were constantly being detonated by wild animals, he
remarked. It was around a quarter to one.

Stauffenberg and Haeften left for the airfield in their
chauffeured car as expeditiously as could be done without causing suspicion. The alarm had still not been raised
when Stauffenberg bluffed his way past the guards on
the gate of the inner zone. He had greater difficulty
leaving the outer perimeter. The alarm had by then been
sounded. He had to telephone an officer, Rittmeister
(captain of cavalry) Leonhard von Möllendorf, who
knew him and was prepared to authorize his passage.
Once out, it was full speed along the bending road to
the airfield. On the way, Haeften hurled away a package
containing the second explosive. The car dropped them
100 yards from the waiting plane, and immediately
turned back. By 1.15 p.m. they were on their way back
to Berlin. They were firmly convinced that no one could
have survived the explosion; that Hitler was dead. Had
they been able to plant the bomb in a concrete bunker,
instead of in the wooden hut where the early-afternoon
conferences were regularly held, they would have been
right.

Hitler had been bent over the heavy oaken table,
propped up on his elbow, chin in his hand, studying
air reconnaissance positions on a map, when the bomb
went off – with a flash of blue and yellow flame and an
ear-splitting explosion. Windows and doors blew out.
Clouds of thick smoke billowed up. Flying glass splinters, pieces of wood, and showers of paper and other

debris flew in all directions. Parts of the wrecked hut were aflame. For a time there was pandemonium. Twenty-four persons had been in the briefing-hut at the time of the explosion. Some were hurled to the floor or blown across the room. Others had hair or clothes in flames. There were cries for help. Human shapes stumbled around – concussed, part-blinded, ear-drums shattered – in the smoke and debris, desperately seeking to get out of the ruins of the hut. The less fortunate lay in the wreckage, some very seriously injured.

Eleven of those who had suffered the worst injuries were rushed to the field hospital, just over two miles away. The stenographer, Dr Heinrich Berger, who had taken the full blast of the bomb, had both legs blown off and died later that afternoon. Colonel Heinz Brandt, Heusinger's right-hand man (and, as it transpired, connected with the conspiracy), lost a leg and died the next day, as did General Günther Korten, chief of the Luftwaffe's general staff, stabbed by a spear of wood. Hitler's Wehrmacht adjutant, Major-General Rudolf Schmundt, lost an eye and a leg, and suffered serious facial burns, eventually succumbing in hospital some weeks later. Of those in the barrack-hut, only Keitel and Hitler avoided concussion; and Keitel alone escaped burst ear-drums.

Hitler had, remarkably, survived with no more than superficial injuries. After the initial shock of the blast, he established that he was all in one piece and could move. Then he made for the door through the wreckage, beating flames from his trousers and putting out the singed hair on the back of his head as he went. He bumped into Keitel, who embraced him, weeping and crying out: 'My Führer, you are alive, you are alive.' Keitel helped Hitler, his uniform jacket torn, his black trousers and beneath them long white underwear in shreds, out of the building. But he was able to walk without difficulty. He immediately returned to his bunker. Dr Morell was summoned urgently. Hitler had a swollen and painful right arm, which he could barely lift, swellings and abrasions on his left arm, burns and blisters on his hands and legs (which were also full of wood-splinters), and cuts to his forehead. But those, alongside the burst ear-drums, were the worst injuries he had suffered. When Linge, his valet, panic-stricken, rushed in, Hitler was composed, and with a grim smile on his face said: 'Linge, someone has tried to kill me.'

Below, Hitler's Luftwaffe adjutant, relatively lightly injured in the explosion, had been composed enough, despite the shock and the lacerations to his face through glass shards, to rush to the signals hut, where he demanded a block on all communications apart from those from Hitler, Keitel, and Jodl. At the same time, Below had Himmler and Göring summoned to Hitler's bunker. Then he made his way there himself. Hitler was sitting in his study, relief written on his face, ready to show off – with a tinge of pride, it seemed – his shredded clothing. His attention had already turned to the question of who had carried out the assassination attempt. According to Below, he rejected suggestions (which he appears initially to have believed) that the bomb had been planted by workers from *Organisation Todt* (OT) – the big construction body named after Hitler's former building, engineering and armaments supremo, Fritz Todt – who were temporarily at Führer Headquarters to complete the reinforcement of the compound against air-raids. By this time, suspicion had turned indubitably to the missing Stauffenberg. The search for Stauffenberg and investigation into the assassination attempt began around 2p.m., though it was not at that point realized that this had been the signal for a general uprising against the regime. Hitler's rage at the army leaders he had always distrusted mounted by the minute. He was ready to wreak terrible vengeance on those whom he saw as stabbing the Reich in the back in its hour of crisis.

*　　*　　*

By this time, Stauffenberg was well on his way back to Berlin. The conspirators there were anxiously awaiting his return, or news of what had happened to him, hesitating to act, still unsure whether to proceed with 'Operation Valkyrie'. The message that Fellgiebel had managed to get through, even before Stauffenberg had taken off from Rastenburg, to Major-General Fritz Thiele, communications chief at Army High Command, was less clear than he thought. It was that something terrible had happened; the Führer was still alive. That was all. There were no details. It was unclear whether the bomb had gone off, whether Stauffenberg had been prevented (as a few days earlier) from carrying out the attack, or whether Stauffenberg had been arrested, whether, in fact, he was even still alive. Further messages seeping through indicated that something had certainly happened in the Wolf's Lair, but that Hitler had survived. Should 'Valkyrie' still go ahead? No contingency plans had been made for carrying out a coup if Hitler were still alive. And without confirmed news of Hitler's death, Fromm, in his position as commander of the reserve army, would certainly not give his approval for the coup. Olbricht concluded that to take any action before hearing definitive news would be to court disaster for all concerned. Vital time was lost. One of the plotters, Hans Bernd Gisevius, connected with the opposition since 1938 and by now an Abwehr agent based in Switzerland who had just returned to Germany, was later scathing about Olbricht's incompetence. 'Leaderless and mindless' was how he described the group in the Bendler-block awaiting Stauffenberg's return. Meanwhile, it had proved only temporarily possible to block communications from the Wolf's Lair. Soon after 4 p.m. that afternoon, before any coup had been started, the lines were fully open again.

Stauffenberg arrived back in Berlin between 2.45 and 3.15 p.m. There was no car to meet him. His chauffeur was waiting at Rangsdorf aerodrome. But Stauffenberg's plane had flown to Tempelhof (or possibly another Berlin aerodrome – this detail is not fully clear), and he had impatiently to telephone for a car to take him and Haeften to Bendlerstraße. It was a further delay. At such a crucial juncture, Stauffenberg did not reach the headquarters of the conspiracy, where tension was at fever-pitch, until 4.30 p.m. Haeften had in the meantime telephoned from the aerodrome to Bendlerstraße. He announced – the first time the conspirators heard the message – that Hitler was dead. Stauffenberg repeated this when he and Haeften arrived in Bendlerstraße. He had stood with General Fellgiebel outside the barrack-hut, he said, and seen with his own eyes first-aid men running to help and emergency vehicles arriving. No one could have survived such an explosion, was his conclusion. However convincing he was for those anxious to believe his message, a key figure, General Fromm, knew otherwise. He had spoken to Keitel around 4 p.m. and been told that the Führer had suffered only minor injuries. That apart, Keitel had asked where, in the meantime, Colonel Stauffenberg might be.

Fromm refused outright Olbricht's request that he should sign the orders for 'Valkyrie'. But by the time Olbricht had returned to his room to announce Fromm's refusal, his impatient chief of staff Colonel Mertz von Quirnheim, a friend of Stauffenberg, and long closely involved in the plot, had already begun the action with a cabled message to regional military commanders, beginning with the words: 'The Führer, Adolf Hitler, is dead.' When Fromm tried to have Mertz arrested, Stauffenberg informed him that, on the contrary, it was he, Fromm, who was under arrest.

By now, several of the leading conspirators had been contacted and had begun assembling in the Bendler-straße. Beck was there, already announcing that he had taken over command in the state; and that Field-Marshal Erwin von Witzleben, former commander-in-chief in France, and long involved in the conspiracy, was now commander-in-chief of the army. General Hoepner, Fromm's designated successor in the coup, dismissed by Hitler in disgrace in early 1942 and forbidden to wear a uniform again, arrived around 4.30 p.m. in civilian clothes, carrying a suitcase. It contained his uniform which he donned once more that evening.

Scenes in the Bendlerstraße were increasingly chaotic. Conspiring to arrange a *coup d'état* in a police state is scarcely a simple matter. But even in the existential circumstances prevailing, much smacked of dilettante organization. Too many loose ends had been left dangling. Too little attention had been paid to small but important details of timing, coordination, and, not least, communications. Nothing had been done about blowing up the communications centre at Führer Headquarters or otherwise putting it permanently out of action. No steps were taken to gain immediate control of radio stations in Berlin and other cities. No broadcast was made by the putschists. Party and SS leaders were not arrested. The master-propagandist, Joseph Goebbels himself, was left at bay. Among the conspirators, too many were involved in issuing and carrying out commands. There was too much uncertainty; and too much hesitation. Everything had been predicated upon killing Hitler. It had simply been taken for granted that if Stauffenberg succeeded in exploding his bomb, Hitler would be dead. Once that premise was called into question, then disproved, the haphazard lines of a plan for the *coup d'état* rapidly unravelled. What was crucial, in the absence of confirmed news of Hitler's demise, was that there were too many regime-loyalists, and too many waverers, with too much to lose by committing themselves to the side of the conspirators.

Despite Stauffenberg's intense avowals of Hitler's

death, the depressing news for the conspirators of his
survival gathered strength. Beck declared that, whatever
the truth of the matter, 'for me this man is dead', and
his further actions would be determined by this. But for
the success of the plot, that was scarcely enough. By
mid-evening, it was increasingly obvious to the insurrectionists that their coup had faltered beyond repair. 'A
fine mess, this,' Field-Marshal Witzleben had muttered
to Stauffenberg, on his arrival around 8p.m. in
Bendlerstraße.

It rapidly became plain in Führer Headquarters that
the assassination attempt was the signal for a military
and political insurrection against the regime. By mid-
afternoon, Hitler had given command of the reserve
army to Himmler. And Keitel had informed army districts that an attempt on the Führer's life had been made,
but that he still lived, and on no account were orders
from the conspirators to be obeyed. Loyalists could be
found even in the Bendlerstraße, the seat of the uprising.
The communications officer there, also in receipt of
Keitel's order, was by the evening, as the conspirators
were becoming more and more desperate, passing on the
message that the orders he was having to transmit on
their behalf were invalid. Fromm's adjutants were meanwhile able to spread the word in the building that Hitler
was still alive, and to collect together a number of officers
prepared to challenge the conspirators, whose already
limited and hesitant support, inside and outside Bendlerstraße, was by now rapidly draining away. Early instances where army units initially supported the coup
dwindled once news of Hitler's survival hardened.

This was the case, too, in Paris. The military commander there, General Karl Heinrich von Stülpnagel, and his subordinate officers had firmly backed the insurrectionists. But the supreme commander in the west, Field-Marshal von Kluge, vacillated as ever. In a vain call from Berlin, Beck failed to persuade him to commit himself to the rising. 'Kluge,' Beck said to Gisevius as he put down the receiver. 'There you have him!' Once he learnt that the assassination attempt had failed, Kluge countered Stülpnagel's orders to have the entire SS, SD (*Sicherheitsdienst*, security service), and Gestapo in Paris arrested, dismissed the general, denounced his actions to Keitel, and later congratulated Hitler on surviving a treacherous attack on his life.

By this time, the events in Berlin had reached their denouement. In the late morning, Goebbels had been hosting a speech about Germany's armaments position, attended by ministers, leading civil servants, and industrialists, given by Speer in the Propaganda Ministry. After the Propaganda Minister had closed the meeting, he had taken Walther Funk and Albert Speer back with him into his study to talk about mobilizing remaining resources within Germany. While they were talking, he was suddenly called to take an urgent telephone call from Führer Headquarters. Despite the swift block on communications, he had his own hot-line to FHQ which, evidently, at this point still remained open. The call was from press chief Otto Dietrich, who broke the news to Goebbels that there had been an attack on Hitler's life. This was within minutes of the explosion taking place. There were few details at this stage, other than that Hitler was alive. Goebbels, told that OT workers had probably been responsible, angrily reproached Speer about the evidently over-casual security precautions that had been taken.

The Propaganda Minister was unusually quiet and pensive over lunch. Somewhat remarkably, in the circumstances, he then retired for his usual afternoon siesta. He was awakened between 2 and 3 p.m. by the head of his press office, Wilfried von Oven, who had just taken a phone call from an agitated Heinz Lorenz, Dietrich's deputy. Lorenz had dictated a brief text – drafted, he said, by Hitler himself – for immediate radio transmission. Goebbels was little taken with the terse wording, and remarked that urgency in transmitting the news was less important than making sure it was suitably couched for public consumption. He gave instructions to prepare an adequately massaged commentary. At this stage, the Propaganda Minister clearly had no idea of the gravity of the situation, that army officers had been involved, and that an uprising had been unleashed. Believing some breach of security had allowed unreliable OT workers to perpetrate some attack, he had been told that Hitler was alive. More than that he did not know. Even so, his own behaviour after first hearing the news, and then during the afternoon, when he attended to regular business and showed unusual dilatoriness in putting out the broadcast urgently demanded from Führer Headquarters, was odd. Possibly he had decided that any immediate crisis had passed, and that he would await further information before putting out any press communiqué. More probably, he was unsure of developments and wanted to hedge his bets.

Eventually, after this lengthy interval, further news from the Wolf's Lair ended his inaction. He rang Speer and told him to drop everything and rush over to his residence, close to the Brandenburg Gate. There he told Speer he had heard from Führer Headquarters that a full-scale military putsch in the entire Reich was under way. Speer immediately offered Goebbels his support in any attempt to defeat and crush the uprising. Within minutes, Speer noticed armed troops on the streets outside, ringing the building. By this time, it was early evening, around 6.30 p.m. Goebbels took one glance and disappeared into his bedroom, putting a little box of cyanide pills – 'for all eventualities' – in his pocket. The fact that he had been unable to locate Himmler made him worried. Perhaps the Reichsführer-SS had fallen into the hands of the putschists? Perhaps he was even behind the coup? Suspicions were rife. The elimination of such an important figure as Goebbels ought to have been a priority for the conspirators. Amazingly, no one had even thought to cut off his telephone. This, and the fact that the leaders of the uprising had put out no proclamation over the radio, persuaded the Propaganda Minister that all was not lost, even though he heard disquieting reports of troops moving on Berlin.

The guard-battalion surrounding Goebbels's house was under the command of Major Otto Ernst Remer, thirty-two years old at the time, a fanatical Hitler-loyalist, who initially believed the fiction constructed by the plotters that they were putting down a rising by disaffected groups in the SS and Party against the Führer. When ordered by his superior, the Berlin City Commandant, Major-General Paul von Hase, to take part in sealing off the government quarter, Remer obeyed without demur. He soon became suspicious, however, that what he had first heard was untrue; that he was, in fact, helping suppress not a putsch of Party and SS leaders against Hitler, but a military coup against the regime by rebellious officers. As luck had it, Lieutenant Hans Hagen, a National Socialist Leadership Officer (*NS-Führungsoffizier*) charged with inspiring the troops with Nazi principles, had that afternoon lectured Remer's battalion on behalf of the Propaganda Ministry. Hagen now used his fortuitous contact to Remer to help undermine the conspiracy against Hitler. Hagen, through the mediation of Deputy Gauleiter of Berlin Gerhard Schach, persuaded Goebbels to speak directly to Remer, to convince him of what was really happening, and to win him over. Hagen then, through an intermediary, sought out Remer, played on the seeds of doubt in his mind about the action in which he was engaged, and talked him into disregarding the orders of his superior, von Hase, and going to see Goebbels. At this point, Remer was still unsure whether Goebbels was part of an internal party coup against Hitler. If he made a mistake, it could cost him his head. However, after some hesitation, he agreed to meet the Propaganda Minister.

Goebbels reminded him of his oath to the Führer. Remer expressed his loyalty to Hitler and the Party, but remarked that the Führer was dead. Consequently, he had to carry out the orders of his commander, Major-

General von Hase. 'The Führer is alive!' Goebbels retorted. 'I spoke with him only a few minutes ago.' The uncertain Remer was visibly wavering. Goebbels offered to let Remer speak himself with Hitler. It was around 7 p.m. Within minutes, the call to the Wolf's Lair was made. Hitler asked Remer whether he recognized his voice. Standing rigidly to attention, Remer said he did. 'Do you hear me? So I'm alive! The attempt has failed,' he registered Hitler saying. 'A tiny clique of ambitious officers wanted to do away with me. But now we have the saboteurs of the front. We'll make short shrift of this plague. You are commissioned by me with the task of immediately restoring calm and security in the Reich capital, if necessary by force. You are under my personal command for this purpose until the Reichsführer-SS arrives in the Reich capital!' Remer needed no further persuasion. All Speer, in the room at the time, could hear was, 'Jawohl, my Führer . . . Jawohl, as you order, my Führer.' Remer was put in charge of security in Berlin to replace von Hase. He was to follow all instructions from Goebbels.

Remer arranged for Goebbels to speak to his men. Goebbels addressed the guard-battalion in the garden of his residence around 8.30 p.m., and rapidly won them over. Almost two hours earlier, he had put out a radio communiqué telling listeners of the attack on Hitler, but how the Führer had suffered only minor abrasions, had received Mussolini that afternoon, and was already back at his work. For those still wavering, the news of Hitler's survival was a vital piece of information. Between 8 and 9p.m. the cordon around the government quarter was lifted. The guard-battalion was by now needed for other duties: rooting out the conspirators in their headquarters in Bendlerstraße. The high-point of the conspiracy had passed. For the plotters, the writing was on the wall.

*   *   *

Some were already seeking to extricate themselves even before Goebbels's communiqué broadcast the news of Hitler's survival. By mid-evening, the group of conspirators in the Bendlerblock, the Wehrmacht High Command building in the Bendlerstraße, were as good as all that was left of the uprising. Remer's guard-battalion was surrounding the building. Panzer units loyal to the regime were closing in on Berlin's city centre. Troop commanders were no longer prepared to listen to the plotters' orders. Even in the Bendlerblock itself, senior officers were refusing to take orders from the conspirators, reminding them of the oath they had taken to Hitler which, since the radio had broadcast news of his survival, was still valid.

A group of staff officers, dissatisfied with Olbricht's increasingly lame explanation of what was happening, and, whatever their feelings towards Hitler, not unnaturally anxious in the light of an evidently lost cause to save their own skins, became rebellious. Soon after 9 p.m., arming themselves, they returned to Olbricht's room. While their spokesman, Lieutenant-Colonel Franz Herber, was talking to Olbricht, shots were fired in the corridor, one of which hit Stauffenberg in the shoulder. It was a brief flurry, no more. Herber and his men pressed into Fromm's office, where Colonel-General Hoepner, the conspirators' choice as commander of the reserve army, Mertz, Beck, Haeften, and the injured Stauffenberg also gathered. Herber demanded to speak to Fromm and was told he was still in his apartment (where he had been kept under guard since the afternoon). One of the rebel officers immediately made his way there, was admitted, and told Fromm what had happened. The guard outside Fromm's door had by now vanished. Liberated, Fromm returned to his office to confront the putschists. It was around 10p.m. when his massive frame appeared in the doorway of his office. He scornfully cast his eye over the utterly dispirited leaders of the insurrection. 'So, gentlemen,' he declared, 'now I'm going to do to you what you did to me this afternoon.'

As Gisevius later pointed out, what the conspirators had done to Fromm had been to lock him in his room and give him sandwiches and wine. Fromm was less naïve. He had his neck to save – or so he thought. He told the putschists they were under arrest and demanded they surrender all weapons. Beck asked to retain his 'for private use'. Fromm ordered him to make use of it immediately. Beck said at that moment he was thinking of earlier days. Fromm urged him to get on with it. Beck put the gun to his head, but only succeeded in grazing himself on the temple. Fromm offered the others a few moments should they wish to write any last words. Hoepner availed himself of the opportunity, sitting at Olbricht's desk; so did Olbricht himself. Beck, meanwhile, reeling from the glancing blow to his head, refused attempts to take the pistol from him, and insisted on being allowed another shot. Even then, he only managed a severe head-wound. With Beck writhing on the floor, Fromm left the room to learn that a unit of the guard-battalion had entered the courtyard of the Bendlerblock. He knew, too, that Himmler, the newly appointed commander of the reserve army, was on his way. There was no time to lose. He returned to his room after five minutes and announced that he had held a court-martial in the name of the Führer. Mertz, Olbricht, Haeften, and 'this colonel whose name I will no longer mention' had been sentenced to death. 'Take a few men and execute this sentence downstairs in the yard at once,' he ordered an officer standing by. Stauffenberg tried to take all responsibility on his own shoulders, stating that the others had been merely carrying out his orders. Fromm said nothing, as the four men were taken to their execution, and Hoepner – initially also ear-marked for execution, but spared for the time being following a private discussion with Fromm – was led out into captivity. With a glance at the dying Beck, Fromm commanded one of the officers to finish him off. The former Chief of the General Staff was unceremoniously dragged into the adjacent room and shot dead.

The condemned men were rapidly escorted downstairs into the courtyard, where a firing-squad of ten men drawn from the guard-battalion was already waiting. To add to the macabre scene, the drivers of the vehicles parked in the courtyard had been ordered to turn their headlights on the little pile of sand near the doorway from which Stauffenberg and his fellow-conspirators emerged. Without ceremony, Olbricht was put on the sand-heap and promptly shot. Next to be brought forward was Stauffenberg. Just as the execution squad opened fire, Haeften threw himself in front of Stauffenberg, and died first. It was to no avail. Stauffenberg was immediately placed again on the sand heap. As the shots rang out, he was heard to cry: 'Long live holy Germany.' Seconds later, the execution of the last of the four, Mertz von Quirnheim, followed. Fromm promptly had a telegram dispatched, announcing the bloody suppression of the attempted coup and the execution of the ringleaders. Then he gave an impassioned address to those assembled in the courtyard, attributing Hitler's wondrous salvation to the work of providence. He ended with a three-fold 'Sieg Heil' to the Führer.

While the bodies of the executed men, along with Beck's corpse which had been dragged downstairs into the yard, were taken off in a lorry to be buried – next day Himmler had them exhumed and cremated – the remaining conspirators in the Bendlerblock (among them Fritz-Dietlof von der Schulenburg, Stauffenberg's brother Berthold, and Yorck von Wartenburg) were arrested. It was around half an hour after midnight.

Apart from the lingering remnants of the coup in Paris, Prague, and Vienna, and apart from the terrible and inevitable reprisals to follow, the last attempt to topple Hitler and his regime from within was over.

*   *   *

Hours earlier on this eventful 20 July 1944, shortly after arriving back in his bunker following the explosion,

Hitler had refused to contemplate cancelling the planned visit of the Duce, scheduled for 2.30 p.m. that afternoon, but delayed half an hour because of the late arrival of Mussolini's train. It was to prove the last of the seventeen meetings of the two dictators. It was certainly the strangest. Outwardly composed, there was little to detect that Hitler had just escaped an attempt on his life. He greeted Mussolini with his left hand, since he had difficulty in raising his injured right arm. He told the shocked Duce what had happened, then led him to the ruined wooden hut where the explosion had taken place. In a macabre scene, amid the devastation, accompanied only by the interpreter, Paul Schmidt, Hitler described to his fellow-dictator where he had stood, right arm leaning on the table as he studied the map, when the bomb went off. He showed him the singed hair at the back of his head. Hitler sat down on an upturned box. Schmidt found a still usable stool amid the debris for Mussolini. For a few moments, neither dictator said a word. Then Hitler, in a quiet voice, said: 'When I go through it all again . . . I conclude from my wondrous salvation, while others present in the room received serious injuries . . . that nothing is going to happen to me.' He was ever more convinced, he added, that it was given to him to lead their common cause to a victorious end.

The same theme, that Providence had saved him, ran through Hitler's address which was transmitted by all radio stations soon after midnight. He had already inquired in mid-afternoon how quickly arrangements for a broadcast could be made, and been told that the earliest was 6 p.m. That was unrealistic. The speech still had to be written, and the afternoon was taken up with Mussolini's visit. Preparations had to be made for the speech to be networked on all radio stations, and recorded. The equipment for the broadcast had to be brought by road from Königsberg, some 75 kilometres away. But the technical crew were not immediately available; they had gone off swimming in the Baltic. Possibly, too, Hitler lost some interest in the idea during the diversions of the day. At any rate, it seems once more to have taken Goebbels's prompting to persuade him of the necessity of a brief address to the German people. It was after midnight before the broadcast eventually took place, followed by addresses by Göring and Dönitz.

Hitler said he was speaking to the German people for two reasons: to let them hear his voice, and know that he was uninjured and well; and to tell them about a crime without parallel in German history. 'A tiny clique of ambitious, unconscionable, and at the same time criminal, stupid officers has forged a plot to eliminate me and at the same time to eradicate with me practically the staff of the German armed forces' leadership.' He likened it to the stab-in-the-back of 1918. But this time, the 'tiny gang of criminal elements' would be 'mercilessly eradicated'. On three separate occasions he referred to his survival as 'a sign of Providence that I must continue my work, and therefore will continue it'.

In fact, as so often in his life, it had not been Providence that had saved him, but luck: the luck of the devil.

* * *

'Now I finally have the swine who have been sabotaging my work for years,' raged Hitler as details of the plot against him started to emerge. 'Now I have proof: the entire General Staff is contaminated.' His long-standing, deep-seated distrust of his army leaders – an inevitable consequence of his ready acceptance of Keitel's fawning description of him following the triumph in France in 1940 as an unparalleled military genius, the 'greatest warlord of all time', together with the inability of the generals, in his eyes, to achieve final victory and, since the first Russian winter, to stave off the endless array of defeats – had found its confirmation. It now seemed blindingly obvious to him why his military plans had encountered such setbacks: they had been sabotaged throughout by the treachery of his army officers. 'Now I know why all my great plans in Russia had to fail in recent years,' he ranted. 'It was all treason! But for those traitors, we would have won long ago. Here is my justification before history' (an indication, too, that Hitler was consciously looking to his place in the pantheon of Teutonic heroes). Goebbels, as so often, echoed Hitler's sentiments. 'The generals are not opposed to the Führer because we are experiencing crises at the front,' he entered in his diary. 'Rather, we are experiencing crises at the front because the generals are opposed to the Führer.' Hitler was convinced of an 'inner blood-poisoning'. With leading positions occupied by traitors bent on destroying the Reich, he railed, with key figures such as General Eduard Wagner (responsible as Quartermaster-General for army supplies) and General Erich Fellgiebel (chief of signals operations at Führer

Headquarters) connected to the conspiracy, it was no wonder that German military tactics had been known in advance by the Red Army. It had been 'permanent treachery' all along. It was symptomatic of an underlying 'crisis in morale'. Action ought to have been taken sooner. It had been known, after all, for one and a half years that there were traitors in the army. But now, an end had to be made. 'These most base creatures who in the whole of history have worn the soldier's uniform, this rabble which has preserved itself from bygone times, must be got rid of and driven out.' Military recovery would follow recovery from the crisis in morale. It would be 'Germany's salvation'.

*   *   *

Vengeance was uppermost in Hitler's mind. There would be no mercy in the task of cleansing the Augean stables. Swift and ruthless action would be taken. He would 'wipe out and eradicate' the lot of them, he raged. 'These criminals' would not be granted an honourable soldier's execution by firing-squad. They would be expelled from the Wehrmacht, brought as civilians before the court, and executed within two hours of sentence. 'They must hang immediately, without any mercy,' he declared. He gave orders to set up a military 'Court of Honour', in which senior generals (including among others Keitel, Rundstedt – who presided – and Guderian) would expel in disgrace those found to have been involved in the plot. Those subsequently sentenced to death by the People's Court, he ordered, were to be hanged in prison clothing as criminals. He spoke favourably of Stalin's purges of his officers. 'The Führer is extraordinarily furious at the generals, especially those of the General Staff,' noted Goebbels after seeing Hitler on 22 July. 'He is absolutely determined to set a bloody example and to eradicate a freemasons' lodge which has been opposed to us all the time and has only awaited the moment to stab us in the back in the most critical hour. The punishment which must now be meted out must have historic dimensions.'

Hitler had been outraged at Colonel-General Fromm's peremptory action in having Stauffenberg and the other leaders of the attempted coup immediately executed by firing-squad. He gave orders forthwith that other plotters captured should appear before the People's Court. The President of the People's Court, Roland Freisler, a fanatical Nazi who, despite early sympathies with the radical Left, had been ideologically committed to the *völkisch* cause since the early 1920s, saw himself – a classical instance of 'working towards the Führer' – pronouncing judgement as the 'Führer would judge the case himself'. The People's Court was, for him, expressly a 'political court'. Under his presidency, the number of death sentences delivered by the Court had risen from 102 in 1941 to 2,097 in 1944. It was little wonder that he had already gained notoriety as a 'hanging judge (*Blutrichter*)'. Recapitulating Hitler's comments at their recent meeting, Goebbels remarked that those implicated in the plot were to be brought before the People's Court 'and sentenced to death'. Freisler, he added, 'would find the right tone to deal with them'. Hitler himself was keen above all – perhaps remembering the leniency of the Munich court in 1924 which had allowed him to turn his trial following the failed putsch into a personal propaganda triumph – that the conspirators should be permitted 'no time for long speeches' during their defence. 'But Freisler will see to that,' he added. 'That's our Vyschinsky' – a reference to Stalin's notorious prosecutor in the show trials of the 1930s.

It took little encouragement from Goebbels to persuade Hitler that Fromm, Stauffenberg's direct superior officer, had acted so swiftly in an attempt to cover up his own complicity. Fromm had, in fact, already been named by Martin Bormann in a circular to the Gauleiter in mid-evening of 20 July as one of those to be arrested as part of the 'reactionary gang of criminals' behind the conspiracy. Following the suppression of the coup in the Bendlerblock and the swift execution of Stauffenberg, Olbricht, Haeften, and Mertz von Quirnheim, Fromm had made his way to the Propaganda Ministry, wanting to speak on the telephone with Hitler. Instead of connecting him, Goebbels had had Fromm seated in another room while he himself telephoned Führer Headquarters. He soon had the decision he wanted. Goebbels immediately had the former commander-in-chief of the Reserve Army placed under armed guard. After months of imprisonment, a mockery of a trial before the People's Court, and a trumped-up conviction on grounds of alleged cowardice – despite the less-than-heroic motive of self-preservation that had dictated his role on centre-stage in the Bendlerblock on 20 July, he was no coward – Fromm would eventually die at the hands of a firing-squad in March 1945.

In the confusion in the Bendlerblock late on the night

of 20 July, it had looked for a time as if other executions would follow those of the coup's leaders (together with the assisted suicide of Beck). But the arrival soon after midnight of an SS unit under the command of Sturm-bannführer Otto Skorzeny – the rescuer of Mussolini from captivity the previous summer – who had been dispatched to the scene of the uprising by Walter Schel-lenberg, head of SD (Security Service) foreign intelli-gence, along with the appearance at the scene of SD chief Ernst Kaltenbrunner and Major Otto Ernst Remer, newly appointed commander of the Berlin guard-battalion and largely responsible for putting down the coup, blocked further summary executions and ended the upheaval. Meanwhile, Himmler himself had flown to Berlin and, in his new temporary capacity as Com-mander-in-Chief of the Reserve Army, had given orders that no further independent action was to be taken against officers held on suspicion.

Shortly before 4 a.m., Bormann was able to inform the Party's provincial chieftains, the Gauleiter, that the putsch was at an end. By then, those arrested in the Bendlerstraße – including Stauffenberg's brother, Berthold, former civil servant and deputy Police Presi-dent of Berlin Fritz-Dietlof von der Schulenburg, leading member of the 'Kreisau Circle' Peter Graf Yorck von Wartenburg, Protestant pastor Eugen Gerstenmaier, and landholder and officer in the Abwehr Ulrich Wilhelm Graf Schwerin von Schwanenfeld – had been led off to await their fate. Former Colonel-General Erich Hoepner, arrested by Fromm but not executed, and Field-Marshal Erwin von Witzleben, who had left the Bendlerstraße before the collapse of the coup, were also promptly taken into custody, along with a number of others who had been implicated. Prussian Finance Minister Popitz, former Economics Minister Schacht, former Chief of Staff Colonel-General Halder, Major-General Stieff, and, from the Abwehr, Admiral Canaris and Major-General Oster were also swiftly arrested. Major Hans Ulrich von Oertzen, liaison officer for the Berlin Defence District (*Wehrkreis* III), who had given out the first 'Valkyrie' orders, blew himself up with a hand grenade. Henning von Tresckow, the early driving-force behind the attempts to assassinate Hitler, killed himself in similar fashion at the front near Ostrow in Poland. General Wagner shot himself. General Fellgiebel refused to do so. 'You stand your ground, you don't do that,' he told his aide-de-camp. Well aware that his arrest was imminent, he spent much of the afternoon, remarkably, at the Wolf's Lair, even congratulated Hitler on his survival, and awaited his inevitable fate.

Those who fell into the clutches of the Gestapo had to reckon with fearsome torture. It was endured for the most part with the idealism, even heroism, which had sustained them throughout their perilous opposition. In the early stages of their investigations, the Gestapo managed to squeeze out remarkably limited information, beyond what they already knew, from those they so grievously maltreated. Even so, as the 'Special Commission, 20 July', set up on the day after the attempted coup under SS-Obersturmbannführer Georg Kießel and soon growing to include 400 officers, expanded its investigations, the numbers arrested rapidly swelled. Kießel was soon able to report 600 persons taken into custody. Almost all the leading figures in the various branches of the conspiracy were rapidly captured, though Goerdeler held out under cover until 12 August. Reports reached Hitler daily of new names among those implicated. His early belief that it had been no more than a 'tiny clique' of officers which had opposed him had proved mistaken. The conspiracy had tentacles stretching further than he could have imagined. He was particularly incensed that even Graf Helldorf, Berlin Police President, 'Old Fighter' of the Nazi Movement, and a former SA leader, turned out to have been deeply implicated. As the list lengthened, and the extent of the conspiracy became clear (all the more so following the remarkably full confession of Goerdeler, anxious to emphasize in the eyes of history the significance of the efforts of the opposition to remove Hitler and his regime), Hitler's fury and bitter resentment against the conservatives – especially the landed aristocracy – who had never fully accepted him mounted. 'We wiped out the class struggle on the Left, but unfortunately forgot to finish off the class struggle on the Right,' he was heard to remark. But now was the worst possible time to encourage divisiveness within the people; the general showdown with the aristocracy would have to wait till the war was over.

Even so, Himmler needed no prompting to take revenge against the families of the plotters, many of them from aristocratic backgrounds. He told the Gauleiter assembled in Posen a fortnight after the attempt on Hitler's life that he would act in accordance with the 'blood-vengeance' traditions of old Germanic law in eradicating 'treasonable blood' throughout the entire clan of the traitors. 'The family of Graf Stauffenberg,' he promised, 'will be wiped out down to its last member.' The Gauleiter applauded. Claus von Stauffenberg's wife, brothers, their children, cousins, uncles, aunts, were all taken into custody. The families of others involved in the plot were similarly imprisoned. Only the end of the war vitiated the fulfilment of Himmler's intention. A full-scale police operation ('*Gewitteraktion*' – 'Storm Action') in late August to round up opponents of the regime – indirectly rather than explicitly a consequence of the plot of 20 July – brought the arrest, in all, of over 5,000 persons. The ferocity of the onslaught against all conceivable glimmers of opposition following the failed bomb-plot was certainly a show of the regime's continued untrammelled capacity for ruthless repression. But the utter ruthlessness now contained more than a mere hint of the desperation that indicated a regime whose days were numbered.

On 7 August, the intended show-trials began at the People's Court in Berlin. The first eight – including Witzleben, Hoepner, Stieff, and Yorck – of what became a regular procession of the accused were each marched by two policemen into a courtroom bedecked with swastikas, holding around 300 selected spectators (including the journalists, hand-picked by Goebbels). There they had to endure the ferocious wrath, scathing contempt, and ruthless humiliation heaped on them by the red-robed president of the court, Judge Roland Freisler. Seated beneath a bust of Hitler, Freisler's face reflected in its contortions extremes of hatred and derision. He

presided over no more than a base mockery of any sem-
blance of a legal trial, with the death sentence a certainty
from the outset. The accused men bore visible signs of
their torment in prison. To degrade them even in physical
appearance, they were shabbily dressed, without collars
and ties, and were handcuffed until seated in the courtroom. Witzleben was even deprived of braces or a belt,
so that he had to hold up his trousers with one hand.
The accused were not allowed to express themselves
properly or explain their motivation before Freisler
cut them short, bawling insults, calling them knaves,
traitors, cowardly murderers. When, for instance, later
in August, Graf Schwerin von Schwanenfeld tried to
point out that his conscience had been wracked by the
many murders he had witnessed in Poland, Freisler
would stand none of it. 'Murders?' he screamed.
'You really are a low scoundrel. Are you breaking down
under this rottenness?' The order had been given – probably by Goebbels, though undoubtedly with Hitler's
authorization – for the court proceedings to be filmed
with a view to showing extracts in the newsreels as
well as in a 'documentary' entitled 'Traitors before the
People's Court'. So loudly did Freisler shout that the
cameramen had to inform him that he was ruining their
sound recordings. Nevertheless, the accused managed
some moments of courageous defiance. For instance,
after the death sentence had predictably been pronounced, General Fellgiebel uttered: 'Then hurry with
the hanging, Mr President; otherwise you will hang
earlier than we.' And Field-Marshal von Witzleben
called out: 'You can hand us over to the hangman. In

three months the enraged and tormented people will call you to account, and will drag you alive through the muck of the street.' Such a black farce were the trials that even Reich Justice Minister Otto Georg Thierack, himself a fanatical Nazi who in his ideological ardour had by this time surrendered practically the last vestiges of a completely perverted legal system to the arbitrary police lawlessness of the SS, subsequently complained about Freisler's conduct.

Once the verdicts had been pronounced, the condemned men were taken off, many of them to Plötzensee Prison in Berlin. On Hitler's instructions they were denied any last rites or pastoral care (though this callous order was at least partially bypassed in practice). The normal mode of execution for civilian capital offences in the Third Reich was beheading. But Hitler had reportedly ordered that he wanted those behind the conspiracy of 20 July 1944 'hanged, hung up like meat-carcasses'. In the small, single-storey execution room, with white-washed walls, divided by a black curtain, hooks, indeed like meat-hooks, had been placed on a rail just below the ceiling. Usually, the only light in the room came from two windows, dimly revealing a frequently used guillotine. Now, however, certainly for the first groups of conspirators being led to their doom, the executions were to be filmed and photographed, as with the filming of the court proceedings presumably in line with Hitler's instructions or those of Goebbels, and the macabre scene was illuminated with bright lights, like a film studio. On a small table in the corner of the room stood a table with a bottle of cognac – for the executioners, not to steady the nerves of the victims. The condemned men were led in, handcuffed and wearing prison trousers. There were no last words, no comfort from a priest or pastor; nothing but the black humour of the hangman. Eye-witness accounts speak of the steadfastness and dignity of those executed. The hanging was carried out within twenty seconds of the prisoner entering the room. Death was not, however, immediate. Sometimes it came quickly; in other cases, the agony was slow – lasting more than twenty minutes. In an added gratuitous obscenity, some of the condemned men had their trousers pulled down by their executioners before they died. And all the time the camera whirred. The photographs and grisly film were taken to Führer Head-quarters. Speer later reported seeing a pile of such photo-graphs lying on Hitler's map-table when he visited the Wolf's Lair on 18 August. SS-men and some civilians, he added, went in to a viewing of the executions in the cinema that evening, though they were not joined by any members of the Wehrmacht. Whether Hitler saw the film of the executions is uncertain; the testimony is contradictory.

Most of the executions connected with the attempted coup followed within the next weeks. Some took place only months later. By the time the blood-letting sub-sided, the death toll of those directly implicated num-bered around 200. But it was Hitler's last triumph.

His initial euphoria at what he took to be his survival ordained by Providence, and at the explanation the 'treachery' of the plotters offered for the causes of Ger-many's military ill-fortune, soon evaporated. The reality of daily setbacks, crises, disasters was too strong even for Hitler to suppress completely. There was little respite. He rapidly had to turn his attention again to military affairs.

However, the Stauffenberg plot left its lasting mark on him. The injuries he had suffered in the bomb blast had been, as we noted, relatively superficial. As if to emphasize his own indestructibility and his manliness in surmounting pain, he made light of his injuries and even joked about them to his entourage. But they were less trivial than Hitler himself implied. Blood was still seeping through the bandages from the skin wounds almost a fortnight after the bomb-attack. He suffered sharp pain in especially the right ear, and his hearing was impaired. He was treated by Dr Erwin Giesing, an ear, nose and throat specialist in a nearby hospital, then by Professor Karl von Eicken, who had removed a throat polyp in 1935 and was now flown in from Berlin. But the ruptured ear-drums, the worst injury, continued bleeding for days, and took several weeks to heal. He thought for some time that his right ear would never recover. The disturbance to his balance from the inner-ear injuries made his eyes turn to the right and gave him a tendency to lean rightwards when he walked. There was also frequent dizziness and malaise. His blood pressure was too high. He looked aged, ill, and strained. Eleven days after the attack on his life, he told those present at the daily military briefing that he was unfit to speak in public for the time being; he could not stand up for long, feared a sudden attack of dizziness, and was also worried about not walking straight. A few weeks later, Hitler admitted to his doctor, Morell, that the weeks since the bomb-attack had been 'the worst of his life' – adding that he had mastered the difficulties 'with a heroism no German could dream of'. Strangely, the trembling in Hitler's left leg and hands practically disappeared following the blast. Morell attributed it to the nervous shock. By mid-September, however, the tremor had returned. By this time, the heavy daily doses of pills and injections could do nothing to head off the long-term deterioration in Hitler's health. At least as serious were the pyschological effects.

His sense of distrust and betrayal now reached paranoid levels. Outward precautions were swiftly taken. Security was at once massively tightened at Führer Head-quarters. At military briefings, all personnel were from now on thoroughly searched for weapons and explosives. Hitler's food and medicines were tested for poison. Any presents of foodstuffs, such as chocolates or caviar (which he was fond of), were immediately destroyed. But the outward security measures could do nothing to alter the deep shock that some of his own generals had turned against him. According to Guderian, whom he appointed as successor to Zeitzler as Chief of the General Staff within hours of Stauffenberg's bomb exploding, 'he believed no one any more. It had already been difficult enough dealing with him; it now became a torture that grew steadily worse from month to month. He frequently lost all self-control and his language grew increasingly violent. In his intimate circle he now found no restraining influence . . .'

Although Hitler stressed that his distrust of his military leaders had been vindicated, and though he had found the scapegoats he needed to explain to himself the setbacks on all fronts, he had never contemplated a plot to overthrow him being hatched by those close to the heart of the regime, especially by officers who, far from straining every sinew for Germany's victory, were doing all they could to undermine the war effort from within. In 1918, according to his distorted vision of the momentous weeks of defeat and revolution, enemies from within had stabbed in the back those fighting at the front. His entire life in politics had been aimed at reversing that disaster, and in eliminating any possible repetition in a new war. Now, a new variant of such treachery had emerged – led, this time, not by Marxist subversives at home threatening the military effort, but by officers of the Wehrmacht who had come close to undermining the war effort on the home front. Suspicion had always been deeply embedded in Hitler's nature. But the events of 20 July now transformed the underlying suspicion into the most visceral belief in treachery and betrayal all around him in the army, aimed once more at stabbing in the back a nation engaged in a titanic struggle for its very survival.

Alongside the thirsting for brutal revenge, the failed bomb-plot gave a further mighty boost to Hitler's sense of walking with destiny. With 'Providence' on his side, as he imagined, his survival was to him the guarantee that he would fulfil his historic mission. It intensified the descent into pure messianism. 'These criminals who wanted to do away with me have no idea what would have happened to the German people,' Hitler told his secretaries. 'They don't know the plans of our enemies, who want to annihilate Germany so that it can never arise again. If they think that the western powers are strong enough without Germany to hold Bolshevism in check, they are deceiving themselves. This war must be won by us. Otherwise Europe will be lost to Bolshevism. And I will see to it that no one else can hold me back or eliminate me. I am the only one who knows the danger, and the only one who can prevent it.' Such sentiments were redolent, through a distorting mirror, of the Wagnerian redeemer-figure, a hero who alone could save the holders of the Grail, indeed the world itself, from disaster – a latter-day Parsifal.

But, once more looking to his own place in history, and looking to the reasons why the path of destiny had led to mounting tragedy for Germany, instead of glorious victory, he found a further reason, beyond the treachery of his generals: the weakness of the people. If Speer can be believed, Hitler gave at this time an intimation that the German people might not deserve him, might have proved weak, have failed its test before history, and thus be condemned to destruction. It was one of the few hints, whether in public or in private, amid the continued outpourings of optimism about the outcome of the war, that Hitler indeed contemplated, even momentarily, the possibility of total defeat.

Whatever the positive gloss he instinctively and insistently placed upon news of the latest setbacks as he continued to play the role of Führer to perfection, he was not devoid of understanding for the significance of the successful landing of the western Allies in Normandy, the dramatic collapse of the eastern front which left the Red Army in striking distance of the borders of the Reich itself, the ceaseless bombing that the Luftwaffe was powerless to prevent, the overwhelming Allied superiority in weaponry and raw materials, and gloomy reports of a mounting, critical fuel shortage. Kluge and Rommel had both urged Hitler to end the war which he could not win. But he continued to dismiss out of hand all talk of suing for peace. The situation was 'not yet ripe for a political solution', he declared. 'To hope for a favourable political moment to do something during a time of severe military defeats is naturally childish and naïve,' he went on, during the military briefing session with his generals on 31 August 1944. 'Such moments can present themselves when you have successes.' But where were the successes likely to materialize? All he could point to was a feeling of certainty that at some point the Allied coalition would break down under the weight of its inner tensions. It was a matter of waiting for that moment, however tough the situation was.

'My task has been,' he continued, 'especially since 1941 under no circumstances to lose my nerve.' He lived, he said, just to carry out this struggle since he knew that it could be won only through a will of iron. Instead of spreading this iron will, the General Staff officers had undermined it, disseminating nothing but pessimism. But the fight would continue, if necessary even on the Rhine. He once more evoked one of his great heroes of history. 'We will under all circumstances carry on the struggle until, as Frederick the Great said, one of our damned opponents is tired of fighting any longer, and until we get a peace which secures the existence of the German nation for the next fifty or a hundred years and' – he was back at a central obsession – 'which, above all, does not defile our honour a second time, as happened in 1918.' This thought brought him directly to the bomb plot, and to his own survival. 'Fate could have taken a different turn,' he continued, adding with some pathos: 'If my life had been ended, it would have been for me personally, I might say, only a liberation from worries, sleepless nights, and severe nervous strain. In a mere fraction of a second you're freed from all that and have rest and your eternal peace. For the fact that I'm still alive, I nevertheless have to thank Providence.'

They were somewhat rambling thoughts. But they were plain enough in meaning: a negotiated peace could not be considered except from a position of strength (which was in realistic terms unimaginable); the only hope was to hold out until the Allied coalition collapsed (but time, and the crass imbalance of material resources, were scarcely on Germany's side); his historic role, as he saw it, was to eradicate any possibility of a second capitulation on the lines of that of November 1918; he alone stood between Germany and calamity; but suicide would bring release for him (whatever the consequences for the German people) within a split second. In Hitler's extraordinary perspective, his historic task was to continue the fight to the point of utter destruction – and even self-destruction – in order to prevent another 'November 1918' and to erase the memory of that 'disgrace' for the nation. It was a task of infinitely greater honour than negotiating a peace from weakness – something which would bring new shame on himself and the German people. It amounted to scarcely less than a realization that the time for a last stand was approaching, and that no holds would be barred in a struggle likely to end in oblivion, where the only remaining monumental vision was the quest for historical greatness – even if Reich and people should go down in flames in the process.

This meant in turn that there was no way out. The failure of the conspiracy to remove Hitler took away the last opportunity of a negotiated end to the war. For the German people, it ensured the near total destruction of their country. Whatever the varied reactions to the events of 20 July and their aftermath, ordinary Germans were exposed over the next eight months to the laying waste of their cities in relentless bombing raids against which there was as good as no defence, to the painful losses of loved ones fighting an obviously futile war against vastly superior enemy forces, to acute privations in the material conditions of their daily lives, and to intensified fear and repression at the hands of a regime that would stop at nothing. The horrors of a war which Germany had inflicted on the rest of Europe were rebounding – if, even now, in far milder form – on to the Reich itself. With internal resistance crushed, and a leadership unable to bring victory, incapable of staving off defeat, and unwilling to attempt to find peace, only total military destruction could bring a release.

For Hitler's countless victims throughout Europe, the advances, impressive though they had been, of the Red Army in the east and the Anglo-American forces in the west and the south, were not yet nearly at the point where they could force an end to the war, and with it the immeasurable suffering inflicted by the Nazi regime. The human misery had, in fact, still not reached its peak. It would rise in crescendo in the months still to come.

*   *   *

Those who had risked their lives in the plot to assassinate Hitler were fully aware that they were acting without the masses behind them. In the event of a successful coup, the conspirators had to hope that a rapid end to the war would win over the vast majority of the population – most of whom had at one time been admirers of Hitler – and that the emergence of a new 'stab-in-the-back legend' (such as had poisoned German politics after the First World War) could be avoided. If they were to fail, the plotters knew they would not have a shred of popular support, that their act would be seen as one of base treachery, and that they could expect to be regarded with nothing but outright ignominy by the mass of the population.

The Nazi leadership was, however, leaving nothing to chance. One Gauleiter, Siegfried Uiberreither, the Nazi leader in Styria, inquired within hours of Stauffenberg's bomb exploding whether public displays of support for Hitler were envisaged. He was told that 'loyalty rallies' were welcomed, and that, in the light of his request, instructions would soon be transmitted to all Gauleiter. These were sent the next day, encouraging huge open-air mass rallies 'in which the joy and satisfaction of the people at the wonderful salvation of the Führer' would be expressed. Such rallies took place over the following days in towns and cities throughout Germany. Hundreds of thousands of ordinary citizens and Wehrmacht representatives 'spontaneously' gave voice to their shock and outrage at the 'foul attempt on the Führer's life' and their relief and happiness that he had survived it.

The sentiments were identical to those recorded in early soundings of opinion taken by the SD and passed on by the Chief of the Security Police Ernst Kaltenbrunner to Martin Bormann after the news of the assassination attempt had spread like wildfire. A first report, compiled on 21 July, announced uniform reactions throughout the German people of 'strongest consternation, shock, deep outrage, and fury'. Even, it was claimed, in districts or among sections of the population known to be critical of Nazism, such sentiments could be registered; not a single comment hinted at sympathy for the planned assassination. In some cities, women were said to have burst into tears in shops or on the streets when they heard what had happened. A remark commonly heard was: 'Thank God the Führer is alive.' Many were prepared to accept Hitler's own version in seeing his survival as a sign of Providence and an indication that, despite all setbacks, the war would end in victory. Very many people, the report added, connected 'mystical, religious notions with the person of the Führer'.

People initially jumped to the conclusion that enemy agents were behind the assassination attempt – an assumption that triggered a new upsurge of hatred against the British. After Hitler's speech – held so late at night that most people were already in bed, but repeated in the early afternoon of 21 July – the fury turned against those seen as traitors within. There was outrage that the attempt on the Führer's life had been carried out by officers of the Wehrmacht, something viewed (as Hitler himself saw it) as the treachery behind Germany's military disasters. Full expectations of a ruthless 'cleansing' of the officer corps were placed in the 'strong man' Heinrich Himmler. Approving comments of Stalin's purges could be heard. And a speech by Robert Ley violently denouncing the aristocracy gave rise to widespread castigation of the 'high-ups', 'big noises', and 'monocle-chaps'. There was resentment that the burdens of 'total war' had not been spread evenly; that too many people had been able to avoid them. Such people needed to be forced into line, however tough the measures were to bring this about. Whatever sacrifices were needed to bring the war to a speedy and victorious end would then be willingly borne.

The failure of the bomb-plot revived strong support for Hitler not only within Germany, but also among soldiers at the front. There was, for instance, a rise in expressions of faith in Hitler among prisoners-of-war captured by the western Allies in Normandy in late July. And the military censor who had examined 45,000 letters of ordinary soldiers from the front in August 1944 commented on 'the high number of joyful expressions about the salvation of the Führer'. There was no compulsion in letters back home even to refer to the attempt on Hitler's life. The pro-Hitler sentiment was doubtless genuine.

Four days after Stauffenberg's bomb had exploded,

the SD reports still stressed the almost unanimous condemnation of the assassination attempt and the joy at
the Führer's survival. There was now, however, a hint
of other voices. 'Only in absolutely isolated cases,' it was
said, 'was the attack not sharply condemned.' A woman
in Halle had been arrested for expressing regret at the
outcome of the bomb-attack. Another woman in Vienna
had remarked that something like that was bound to
happen because the war was lasting so long. But – so the
SD claimed – even 'politically indifferent' sectors of the
population reacted heatedly against such comments.

The backlash of support for Hitler and ferocity of
condemnation of those who had tried to kill the Führer,
as mirrored in the SD's reports, had, as we have noted,
been fully anticipated by the plotters themselves in the
event of their failure. It highlighted the extensive reser-
voir of Hitler's popularity that still existed and could be
tapped to bolster the regime at a critical time, despite
the increasingly self-evident catastrophic course of the
war. The Führer cult was far from extinguished.

But Hitler's popularity had unquestionably waned
over the previous two years. He had personally been
drawn increasingly into the blame for the miseries of a
war almost certain to end in defeat. It is hard to imagine,
therefore, that the unanimity of feelings of joy at his
survival recorded by the SD could have been an accurate
reflection of the views of the German people as a whole.
The SD was unquestionably registering widely expressed
opinion, indeed indicating a real upsurge in pro-Hitler
feeling. But the opinions the SD's informants were able
to hear would doubtless have been those emanating

in the main from regime-loyalists, Nazi fanatics, and those anxious to demonstrate their support or dispel any suspicions that they might be critical of Hitler. People with less positive views were well advised to keep them to themselves – at such a critical juncture quite especially. As war-fortunes had worsened, punishment for incautious remarks had become more draconian. Expressing out loud in late July 1944 regret that Hitler was still alive was as good as suicidal. Some people did take risks. A Berlin tram conductor ventured a brief but pointed commentary on Goebbels's radio address on 26 July, in which the Propaganda Minister had casti-gated the plotters. 'It makes you want to throw up,' the tram conductor remarked. He seems to have got away with it.

Critical sentiments could be expressed safely, how-ever, only in privacy, or among trusted family or friends. One boy, for instance, just sixteen at the time, confided on 21 July 1944 in the remarkable diary that he kept in the attic of a house near Hamburg: 'Assassination attempt on Hitler! Yesterday, an attack on Hitler with explosives was carried out in his study. Unfortunately, as if by a miracle the swine was unharmed . . . Last night at 1 a.m. Hitler gave a speech on the radio. It's very noticeable that Hitler repeated six times that it's only a matter of "a tiny clique". But his extensive measures give the lie to these claims. You don't need to put in an entire army to wipe out "a tiny cabal".' The boy kept the diary to himself, not even showing it to his parents.

Another diary entry, from a one-time Hitler-loyalist whose former enthusiasm had turned cold, confined

itself to the cynically ambiguous comment: 'Assassination attempt on the Führer. "Providence" has saved
him, and therefore we can believe in victory.' Letters
to loved ones were also best 'coded' for safety. One
well-educated German, for years a strong critic of
Nazism, writing on 21 July from Paris to his Canadian
wife in Germany, remarked about the events of the previous day: 'For some people it can hardly have been a
good night, but we must be thankful that the affair ended
as it did. For this war, as I have always pointed out,
can only be brought to the desired conclusion by Adolf
Hitler!'

Signs that there were voices beyond the unanimous
condemnation summarized by the SD, and that the
silence of a large majority of the population was evocative, could even be found in official reports from provincial localities. One such report from Upper Bavaria
frankly admitted that 'part of the population would
have welcomed the success of the assassination attempt
because in the first instance they would have hoped for
an earlier end to the war from it'. Another report relayed
the perilous remark uttered by a woman, hidden in the
gloom in the corner of a dark air-raid shelter: 'If only
they'd have got him.'

At the front, too, opinion about the bomb-plot was
more divided than appearances suggested. Implying any
regret that Hitler had survived was to court disaster.
Letters home had to pass through the control of the
censor and might be intercepted. It was safest to keep
quiet. So it is remarkable that there was even a slight
increase in criticism of the regime in August 1944, and

even more telling that some letters risked extreme retribution for the sender. One soldier was lucky. His letter home on 4 August escaped the attention of the censor. It ran: 'You write in your letter of the attack on the Führer. Yes, we heard of it even on the same day. Unfortunately, the gents had bad luck. Otherwise there'd already be a truce, and we'd be saved from this mess.' In other instances, the censor picked up similar bold comments. The death sentence for the writer of the letter was then an almost certain consequence.

As the reactions to the bomb-plot revealed, the bonds of the German people to Hitler, if greatly loosened, were far from broken in mid-1944. The failure of Stauffenberg's attempt had prompted an outpouring of support for Hitler which unquestionably strengthened the regime for a time. The feeling that to attempt to kill the head of state, and at a time when the nation was fighting for its very existence, was a heinous crime was far from confined to Nazi fanatics. The Catholic sector of the population, for instance, recognized for its lukewarm backing for a regime which since its inception had conducted its attritional campaign against the Church, was also prominently represented in the huge demonstrations of loyalty to Hitler in late July. Both major denominations – important formative influences on opinion – condemned the attempt to kill Hitler even after the war. And as late as the early 1950s, a third of those questioned in opinion surveys still criticized the attack on Hitler's life on 20 July 1944. But above all, the voices captured by the SD in the first days after the assassination attempt were those of the dwindling masses of continued loyal believers in the Führer. They had spoken loudly for the last time. What proportion of the population (or even of a Nazi Party with a nominal membership by this time of over 8 million Germans) they represented can only be guessed at; but they constituted by now almost certainly a minority – if still a controlling minority with massive repressive capacity.

Even some of the SD's own provincial stations were providing, within weeks of the explosion in the Wolf's Lair, blunt indicators of the collapse in Hitler's popularity. A devastating report on 8 August from the SD office in Stuttgart, for instance, began by stating that for the overwhelming majority of the population in that area it was not a question of whether Germany would win the war, but only whether they would be ruled by the Anglo-Americans or the Russians. Beyond a small number of Party activists and a tiny section of the population, no one thought there would be a miracle. People read into Hitler's speech on the night after Stauffenberg's bomb-attack the exact opposite of what was intended. It was now plain, they said, that Göring, Goebbels, and other leading men in the regime had lied to them in claiming that time was on Germany's side, armaments production was rising, and the day of a return to the offensive backed by new, decisive weapons was close at hand. They had now heard in the Führer's own words that his work had been sabotaged for years. In other words, people were saying: 'The Führer is admitting that time has previously not been on our side, but running against us. If such a man as the Führer has been so thoroughly deceived,' the summary of prevailing opinion continued, 'then he is either not the genius that he has been depicted as, or, knowing that saboteurs were at work, he intentionally lied to the German people, which would be just as bad, for, with such enemies within, war production could never have been raised, and we could never gain victory.' The consequence of such thoughts was made explicit: 'The most worrying aspect of the whole thing is probably that most comrades of the people, even those who up to now have believed unshakeably, have lost all faith in the Führer.'

As the autumn wore on and Hitler, after his brief return for a final time to the centre of people's attention, again faded from most people's daily consciousness, attitudes against him in the same region hardened still further. On 6 November, the Stuttgart SD office recorded opinion which could in variants, it suggested, be frequently heard: 'It's always claimed that the Führer has been sent to us from God. I don't doubt it. The Führer was sent to us from God, though not in order to save Germany, but to ruin it. Providence has determined the destruction of the German people, and Hitler is the executor of this will.'

Sometimes, irrational belief was all that was left. A teenage girl, writing in her diary at the end of August and in early September 1944, saw blow following blow in Germany's war effort: the attack on the Führer's life, advances of the western Allies, constant German retreat on the eastern front, the incessant bombing, and the collapse of the Reich's alliance-partners. 'On one side there is victory, which is becoming ever more doubtful, and on the other Bolshevism,' she wrote. 'But then:

rather sacrifice everything, absolutely everything, for victory, than for Bolshevism. If that should come, then you shouldn't think further. What would I still go to school for if I'm going to end up in Siberia? What for? What for? A whole number of questions line up like this. But if we all wanted to think in this way, there would be no hope left. So, head high. Trust in our will and our leadership!!!'

As this diary entry suggests, the fear of Bolshevism was by now among the most central cohesive elements sustaining support for the German war effort and militating against any collapse of morale at home. Even so, as the news of defeats, destruction, and desertion of allies mounted without relief, and as losses of property and possessions, homes and loved ones piled misery on misery, the first signs of disintegration were visible. The German greeting, 'Heil Hitler', was increasingly replaced by 'Good morning', 'Good day', or, in south Germany, 'Grüß Gott'. The evacuation of the Aachen area – the old seat of Charlemagne's empire, where the Allies had broken through – in early September was accompanied by 'a more or less panic-type of flight by the German civilian population', according to a report to Himmler. Wehrmacht reports from the western front spoke later in the month of mounting lack of discipline and indications of disintegration among the troops, with increasing numbers of desertions, reflected in a sharp rise in draconian punishment meted out by military courts.

Some of the deserters in the west made their way to Cologne. This great city on the Rhine had by now been largely bombed into dereliction – though, amazingly, its magnificent Gothic cathedral was still standing – with much of its population evacuated. Amid the rubble and the ruins, in the cellars of burnt-out buildings, forms of opposition to the Nazi regime approaching partisan activity emerged. Here, heterogeneous groups of deserting soldiers, foreign workers – now forming around 20 per cent of the Reich's work force and presenting the Nazi authorities with increasing worries about insurrection – members of dissident bands of disaffected youth (known picturesquely as 'Edelweiß Pirates'), and the Communist underground organization (infiltrated and smashed many times but always managing to replenish itself) blended together in the autumn of 1944 into short-lived but, for the regime, troublesome resistance. The Gestapo recorded some two dozen small resistance groups of up to twenty individuals, and one large body of around 120 persons. They stole food, broke into Wehrmacht camps and depots to get weapons, and organized minor forms of sabotage. It came on occasion to shoot-outs with camp guards and police. Their actions were politically directed: they killed, among others, several Gestapo men, including the head of the Cologne Gestapo, an SA man, and a Nazi Party functionary. In all, twenty-nine killings were attributed to them by the Gestapo. Attacks on the Hitler Youth and other Nazi formations by the 'Edelweiß Pirates' were commonplace. With the explosives they acquired, their intention was to blow up the Gestapo headquarters and the city's law-courts, and to shoot a leading attorney and several members of the Party organization. Possibly, had the Allied advance in the west not slowed, the quasi-partisan

The Driving Forces

1. Henning von Tresckow

2. Claus von Stauffenberg

Early Opponents

3. Ludwig Beck as Chief of
General Staff, *c.* 1937

4. Carl Goerdeler as Mayor of Leipzig, 1934 (*not in uniform, with Winifred
Wagner, Hitler, Martin Mutschmann, Gauleiter of Saxony and Joseph Goebbels*)

Army Group Central Plotters

5. Rudolph-Christoph Freiherr von Gersdorff

6. Fabian von Schlabrendorff

Disaster on the Eastern Front

7. Smashed up Waffen-SS equipment

8. Thousands of German prisoners being marched through Moscow,
17 July 1944

The Bomb

9. Ruins of the briefing room

10. Hitler with the injured Major-General Walter Scherff, the official
Wehrmacht war chronicler

The Aftermath

11. Otto Ernst Remer

12. Friedrich Fromm

13. Werner von Haeften

14. Albrecht Ritter Mertz von Quirnheim

15. Friedrich Olbricht

The Trial

16. Roland Freisler

17. Peter Graf Yorck von Wartenburg

18. Adam von Trott

The Brutal Reckoning

19. SD-Chief Ernst Kaltenbrunner (*foreground*) and leading officials from the Propaganda Ministry, Hans Hinkel and Werner Naumann, attending the trial

20. The execution room in Plötzensee

activity in Cologne might have spread to other cities in the Rhine and Ruhr region. The problems of combating it would then have magnified. As it was, the Gestapo, aided by Wehrmacht units, was able to strike back with devastating effect in the autumn. The resistance groups did not give up without a fight. One group waged an armed battle for twelve hours before the ruined cellar which served as its 'fortress' was blown up. Another group defended itself with hand grenades and a machine-gun, finally breaking through a police cordon and escaping. By the time the Gestapo were finished, however, some 200 members of the resistance groups had been arrested, the groups themselves totally destroyed, their leaders executed, and many other members imprisoned.

Had the Stauffenberg bomb-plot succeeded, it is possible that the types of grass-roots political activism experienced in Cologne could have swelled into a revolutionary ferment from a base in western Germany. But many – and quite conflicting – scenarios could be imagined had Hitler been assassinated on 20 July. The actual outcome was that resistance from below – from Communists, Socialists, youth rebels, foreign workers, deserting soldiers and others – was, whatever the continued courage of those involved, robbed of any prospect of success. The regime had been challenged internally. But the blow to its heart had not proved lethal. It now reacted with all the ferocity at its disposal. At least for the time being, it was able to regroup and reconsolidate, delaying the end for several more months, prolonging the agony of millions caught up in the intensifying maelstrom of death and destruction. Hitler and the Nazi leadership had survived. But there was no way leading from the self-destructive path on which they were embarked.

For the ordinary German, too, there was no way out. It was taken for granted that the regime was finished. The only hope was that the British and Americans would hold off the Bolsheviks. The most common reactions, as yet another war winter loomed, were apathy, resignation, fatalism. 'It's all the same to me. I can't judge the situation any longer. I'll just work further in my job, wait, and accept what comes' – this approach, reported by the regional agencies of the Propaganda Ministry in autumn 1944, was said to be prevalent not just with 'the man on the street', but also among Party members and even functionaries, some of whom were no longer wanting to wear their Party insignia. It was a clear sign that the end was on the way.

I

Fabian von Schlabrendorff's Account of the Assassination Attempt of 13 March 1943

Taken from the memoirs of Schlabrendorff (1907–80), a close associate of Tresckow, who had direct insight into plans to kill Hitler in 1943 within Army Group Centre.

When Hitler arbitrarily started the war against Poland on September 1, 1939, three decisive prerequisites had been fulfilled for the undertaking of a coup d'état against Hitler with the prospect of success:

1. Connections with numerous forces outside of Germany had been established, a project which brought into the range of possibility an interplay of the circles fighting against National Socialism all over the world.

2. The resistance movement based on Christian foundations had made connections with the military. Thereby it had reached out to grasp the one tool by which the death blow against National Socialism could be delivered.

3. Because of the outbreak of the war the army as the instrument chosen for action was freed from the bonds imposed on it by conditions of peace and could act . . .

*　　*　　*

Up to 1942 Tresckow had not stayed idle. On the one side he had doubled his efforts to make his commander-in-chief, Field Marshal von Kluge, receptive to the idea of removing Hitler. Kluge, as commander-in-chief of an army group, should – that was the basic thought – place himself on the side of the coup d'état from the beginning. By so doing he would have exerted an enormous pressure on all undecided commanders at the front and also in the reserve army. At the same time he could begin with rolling back the East Front into a shorter and thereby more defensible rear position, which had been demanded by the general staff again and again but was refused by Hitler. All other groups of the army would necessarily have had to join this enterprise. Tresckow also endeavored to create the practical prerequisites for the priming that he had in mind. The practical prerequisites consisted in the following: Hitler had to be induced to leave his headquarters in East Prussia and to visit the staff of the middle army group, which at that time was located in a forest camp west of Smolensk. Tresckow wanted to bring Hitler to surroundings which would be strange to him and well-known to us in order to create an atmosphere favorable to the priming. His years-long acquaintance with Hitler's chief adjutant, General Schmundt, was useful for Tresckow's efforts. Schmundt was a convinced adherent of Hitler, but he was not clever enough to perceive that Tresckow's request that he should have Hitler visit Kluge's headquarters was only a military pretence in order to touch off a political act of the greatest consequence. Thus it came about that Hitler announced that he would visit Field-Marshal von

Kluge in Smolensk during the first days of March 1943.

At first the matter rested with this announcement. Hitler acted as so often in such situations. He announced his visit, only to cancel it shortly before the set date. Thus it went to and fro a few times until Hitler arrived in Smolensk on March 13, 1943, by plane. If Kluge had been ready at that time to follow his good judgment, the tyrant would have been removed in March 1943. With the agreement of Kluge the removal of Hitler would not have been too difficult. Thus the army group had created a cavalry regiment whose commander, Baron von Boeselager, was one of our number. The officer corps was so selected that Boeselager, who combined in himself both military prudence and spirited pugnacity, could have acted. But Kluge had the comprehension but not the will. In a word: he hesitated. Again and again he objected that neither the world nor the German soldier would understand such a deed at this time. One would have to wait till the events of themselves suggested Hitler's removal. Thus it was not possible right from the beginning to make use of the command apparatus of the army group for the planned plot.

For that reason Tresckow decided to waste no more time, but to play the part himself. We hoped that after the assassination had been carried out Kluge would no longer refuse but – faced with accomplished facts – would follow his basically right judgment. In order to make action easier for him and the whole military command staff, Tresckow planned the following: he did not want to shoot Hitler, but instead to remove him during the flight by means of a bomb smuggled into his plane;

and so avoid the odium of an assassination by simulating an airplane accident . . .

After we had successfully finished our tests we undertook the immediate preparations themselves. For them Tresckow had the following plan: in order to be quite sure of the effect we took not one but two explosive charges, and made a parcel of them which had the shape of two cognac bottles. Then we had to arrange the parcel in such a way that is was possible to operate the fuse by hand without destroying the wrapper. I myself took charge of the thus-prepared parcel on March 13, 1943, and locked it in a box which was only accessible to me. Meanwhile Kluge and Tresckow rode to Smolensk airport to meet Hitler . . .

During the meal Tresckow spoke to one of Hitler's companions, and asked him whether he would be willing to take along a small parcel on his way back to headquarters, consisting of two bottles of cognac, addressed to General Stieff in the army high command. Hitler's companion agreed. In the early morning, as agreed, I phoned the colleague who had been named to me by Oster, Captain Gehre in Berlin, and gave him the password about the immediately imminent priming. This way had been previously agreed upon. From Gehre it went to Dohnanyi and from him to Oster. Their task was to make the immediately necessary preparations for the second step.

After the lunch in Smolensk Hitler returned to the airport, accompanied by Kluge and Tresckow. At about the same time I got the bomb and took it to the airport. Here I waited until Hitler had said good-bye to the officers of the middle army group and was about to board the plane. At that moment I threw the fuse and after a sign from Tresckow handed the parcel to Colonel Brandt. He boarded the same plane with Hitler. Shortly afterwards, Hitler's plane and the plane of some of his accompanying personnel took off in the direction of East Prussia, accompanied by several fighters. We rode back to our quarters. From there I phoned Gehre in Berlin once again and gave him the additional password that informed Dohnanyi and Oster about the starting of the priming.

It was known to us that Hitler's plane was equipped with special security measures. It consisted of several isolated cabins. Hitler's seat was armored and had a contrivance with the help of which a direct parachute jump was possible. In our opinion the explosive charge would be enough to tear the whole plane apart. If, contrary to expectation, this should not happen, at least such an essential part of the plane would be torn away by the explosion that it would crash.

By our time calculations we expected the plane to crash shortly before it reached Minsk, and we supposed that a report on the crash would be sent by one of the accompanying fighters to its air force duty station. Instead of that, nothing happened.

After more than two hours the message arrived that Hitler's plane had had a smooth landing at the Rastenburg airport and that he had reached his headquarters. So it was clear that the planned assassination had failed.

We did not know to what to attribute this failure. Again I phoned Gehre, and I gave him the password about the failure of the plot. Then Tresckow and I discussed what to do. We were very much excited. It was bad enough that the plot itself had failed, but discovery of the bomb would mean our exposure.

After careful consideration Tresckow decided to phone Colonel Brandt. He asked him not to hand over the parcel to General Stieff, but to keep it till the next day, as a mix-up had occurred. From his answer we realized that the bomb camouflaged as a parcel containing two cognac bottles had not yet been discovered. We had to prevent its being handed on to General Stieff because at this time he was not yet a member of the conspiracy.

Under a military pretext I rode to headquarters in one of the regular courier planes the following day, looked up Colonel Brandt in the operations department there, and exchanged the parcel with the bomb in it for another parcel that really contained two bottles of cognac for General Stieff . . .

2

The Kreisau Circle's 'Principles for the New Order in Germany', 9 August 1943

A key statement of the group's ideals, directed at the restoration of peace, freedom and justice, composed as a result of three gatherings of the Kreisau Circle in previous months, by one of its leading figures, Helmuth James Graf von Moltke (1907–45).

The Government of the German *Reich* sees in Christianity the basis for the ethical and religious revival of our people, for the conquest of hatred and lies, for the creation anew of the European community of people.

The starting point lies in the pre-ordained contemplation by the human being of the divine order which yields to him his inner and outer existence. Only if there is success in making this order the measure of the relations between individuals and communities can the disorder of our time be overcome and a real condition of peace be achieved. The inner reorganization of the *Reich* is the basis for the carrying-through of a just and permanent peace.

In the collapse of a power formation which is without

roots and is based exclusively on the mastery of technique, European humanity is faced with a common task. The way to its solution lies in the decisive and active implementation of the Christian substance of life. The government of the *Reich* is therefore determined to realize the following goals, which cannot be renounced either inwardly or outwardly, with all the means at its disposal:

1. Justice, fallen and trampled, must be restored, and must be made supreme over all orders of human life. This justice, under the protection of conscientious, independent judges who are free from fear of men, will be the basis for the future moulding of peace.

2. Freedom of faith and conscience is guaranteed. Existing laws and regulations which offend against these principles are at once abolished.

3. The casting away of the totalitarian restraints on conscience and the recognition of the inviolable dignity of the human being are foundations of the law and of the desired peaceful order of things. Everyone cooperates with full responsibility in the various social, political and international spheres of life. The right of work and property stands under public protection without regard to race, nationality or creed.

4. The basic unit of peaceful community life is the family. It stands under public protection, which shall ensure, along with education, the tangible goods of life; food, clothing, a home, a garden and health.

5. Work must be arranged in such a way that it fosters rather than stunts the enjoyment of personal responsibility. To this belongs, besides the shaping of the material

conditions of work and the improvement of education in professional training, an effective co-responsibility of each person in the enterprise and beyond that in the general economic relations to which his work contributes. Thus he may cooperate in the creation of a healthy and lasting order of life, which will enable the individual, his family and the communities to achieve their organic fulfilment within balanced spheres of economic activity. The ordering of the economy must ensure that these basic requirements are met.

6. The personal political responsibility of everyone requires his co-determining participation in the self-administration of the small and surveyable communities, which are to be revived. Rooted firmly in them, his co-determination in the state and in the community at large must be secured by self-elected representatives, and thus there must be conveyed to him a living conviction of his co-responsibility for political events in general.

7. The special responsibility and faithfulness which each individual owes to his national origin, his language, the spiritual and historical tradition of his people has to be respected and protected. However, it must not be misused for the accumulation of political power, for the degradation, persecution and suppression of foreign peoples. The free and peaceful development of national culture can no longer be made consonant with the maintenance of an individual state's absolute sovereignty. Peace demands the creation of an order which encompasses the individual states. As soon as the free agreement of all peoples involved is guaranteed, the supporters of this order must also have the right to demand

from each individual obedience, respect, if necessary also the risking of life and property, for the highest political authority of the community of peoples.

3

Carl Goerdeler's Peace Plan,
late summer to autumn 1943

*Extracts from one of a number of
programmatic statements by Goerdeler
(1886–1945), the leading figure in the
conservative civilian resistance, aimed at
the renewal of political life based upon law
and moral values, and strongly advocating in
this memorandum the need for continued
German strength as a bulwark against the
power of Russia.*

We start with these premises:

1. That Germany must be morally and materially strong for the sake of the German people, the peoples of Europe, and the peace of the world.
2. That between England and Russia there are conflicts of interest, from East Asia to the Mediterranean, from the Mediterranean to the North Atlantic, that are based on circumstances.
3. That Europe needs security against the superior force of Russia.

4. That at present this security can only be underwritten for any length of time by England or Germany.
5. That it is doubtful whether America will make available permanent forces to provide this security.
6. That it therefore is reasonable and necessary to implement the natural community of interests between England and Germany, as fulfilling all the prerequisites.
7. That this implementation can only be possible if the European peoples come together in an eternal league of peace in freedom and independence, with neither Germany nor any other power claiming supremacy.
8. That no white nationality may contribute to enabling Japan to expand at the expense of other white nationalities or of China.
9. And that, moreover, the whole world is in need of economic cooperation in order to bring its finances into order, to assure employment, and to re-establish the foundation of prosperity.

Germany must restore justice and decency again at home. She owes this to her own honour and to others. She can regain her spiritual health only if she herself punishes offenders against the law, and also the offences against international law. Therefore an urgent admonition must be sounded against any thought of leaving this punishment to be administered by a third party or by an international court. Even the Germans who hate and despise the violation of Germany's good name by Germans, and who are ready to impose every just penalty – or, rather, precisely those Germans – will persistently reject participation in the administration of such penalties by a third party. The feelings of the victimized peoples are quite understandable to these Germans, in view of the monstrous crimes, unique in history, that Hitler and his henchmen have committed. But reason, and a responsibility toward the future, demand that these feelings be kept in check. Anyone in the world, of course, and any government, is free to lodge a charge against German criminals, and the complainant will be informed about the measures that are taken thereupon. Nor can there be any objection to the presence of an official representative of the victimized nation during the public trial. Moreover, the public nature of such trials will be guaranteed, thus ensuring an opportunity to verify that they are genuine. After the enormous misfortune into which Hitler has plunged the German people, there is no doubt that the German courts will tend more to severity than to softness.

The importance of Germany's becoming sufficiently strong again follows from the necessity of securing the German *Reich* at least against the permanent pressure of the gigantic Russian power. This in turn involves the necessity of preserving the territorial existence of Germany that has proved reasonable and necessary through history.

Any plan to divide Germany will create repeated tensions in Germany and therefore in Europe. After all, Germany does lie in the middle of the Continent. The following come into consideration as Germany's borders: In the East: approximately the *Reich* borders of 1914.

In the South: the boundary recognized in the Munich

conference of 1938, including Austria; moreover, South Tyrol, a purely German region, should return to Germany, up to the border of Bozen-Meran. The Italian control has only created resentment and backwardness there.

In the West: The Alsace–Lorraine question is very hard to solve. There will be no rest if Alsace–Lorraine in its old form is awarded to either Germany or France. There are two other possibilities:

(a) Alsace–Lorraine can become an autonomous country, perhaps along the lines of Switzerland.

(b) Or a neutral commission can determine the language boundary as it existed in 1918 and 1938. The French–German border would then be located between these two lines. In this second case Germany would be conceding a far-reaching self-administration to Alsace–Lorraine. This concession is based as much on existing circumstances as on our convictions and goals.

In the North: The proper border with Denmark should be determined in a way similar to that followed in the West.

In any event, the internal European borders will play an ever less important part, within the European federation towards which we must strive.

This territorial continuity of the German *Reich* presupposes an understanding with Poland. As far as can be seen now, the continued existence of Poland depends on whether the German front in the East maintains the eastern border of Poland as of 1938. If the front collapses, Poland is lost to Russia. We understand very well the indignation and the bitterness of the Polish people after all that has happened. We would feel the same. But here again a responsibility toward the future demands that such feelings be prevented from playing a prevailing role. They must be subordinated to orderly processes: punishment of the criminals, and restitution by co-operation. Poland can receive a substitute for West Prussia and Posnania through a federal union with Lithuania. This would benefit both peoples, and Poland would have her access to the sea. Such a union has in fact existed in earlier centuries; it broke up over dynastic questions. Such tensions no longer exist today, or are surmountable. Moreover, there is the possibility of guaranteeing Poland connections with world trade and traffic via the German harbours. In the future, such relationships will no longer be restricted to military arrangements. For all the peoples of Europe will survive or go under, depending on whether lasting peace is won.

Thus it is to be hoped that gradually, in the wake of these terrible and painful experiences, the relationship between Germany and Poland will find its adjustment. In any case, we will be ready to extend every possible aid to Poland now, in the healing of its wounds, and in the future.

A restitution of the damage that has been inflicted on the European and other peoples through Hitlerism is unthinkable. Even before the present war, Hitler had involved Germany in enormous debts. The admiration that other peoples bestowed on Hitler's skill in this area of operations was fatal for the German people. Germany shares with the whole world the immense burden of debts from this wretched war. But the destruction caused by the war is already more extensive in Germany than in any other part of Europe. Therefore it is physically impossible for Germany to undertake reconstruction in other countries, along with the reconstruction at home, which will take generations.

We therefore suggest a project for the sake of both emotional relaxation and tangible help to Europe: a European community undertaking of reconstruction, in which each European state would participate according to its resources.

We need not say anything about the conflicts of interest between England and Russia; they are there. In the 19th Century they were neutralized within the European balance of power. In spite of that balance, there were armed conflicts – as, for example, the Crimean War. In 1918 England could accept the thoughtlessly humiliating treatment of Germany, because the might of Russia seemed to have been eliminated for a long time to come. But now Russia's recuperation cannot be doubted. Certainly Russia, too, is severely weakened by this war. But the Russian people, close to nature as they are, compensate for such losses more quickly than the more sensitive European peoples can.

At present Russia is governed by a uniformly Bolshevist system. Even the Russians cannot close their eyes to the fact that Bolshevism kills all human aspiration and endeavour. Accordingly, they have increasingly diluted Communism. But that comes only after a people under Communism has had its own bitter experience with the system. If the Russia of today gains supremacy over Europe, the Central and West European peoples, weak-

ened by war, moved by emotions, facing almost unsur-
mountable tasks, will fall prey to radical Bolshevism.
That would be the death of European culture, and of
Europe as an entity. It would also be a great danger to
England. Yet Russia will be still more dangerous if she
gradually finds her way back to the true laws of economics and statesmanship. For then her power will
become constantly greater. Russia is the sole power on
earth that can threaten the British Empire without a big
fleet. It is of course England's own affair to examine
this situation and then draw any conclusion that she
considers to be necessary in her own interest. We can
only give our opinion: that all European peoples to the
west of Russia must protect themselves against Russian
supremacy and hegemony.

Neither France nor Italy nor a union of the smaller
peoples can at present guarantee this security. Germany
can still do it, if she sends the criminals to the devil in
good time, punishes them, and is permitted by England
and America to liquidate the war short of collapse. An
obstacle to that development is the demand for unconditional surrender. . . .

Germany is pleased to note that America will continue
to concern herself with European affairs after this war.
Germany is convinced that it is a fairy tale to maintain
that America intends to obtain a foothold in Europe or
in Africa. Nor do we seriously believe that in America
one thinks with all seriousness of administering Germany with American forces, or of reforming her schools
and making Germany healthy again. If we Germans who
strive to save our fatherland from moral and physical

collapse were materialists without a conscience, then we could calmly accept this American intention, which has been communicated to us more than once. For it would soon be shown that it was expensive for America, dangerous, and finally unworkable. That is to say, America would take over the total responsibility for the misery in Germany and for Germany's reconstruction, and would thereby relieve Germany of the burden. But on idealistic grounds we firmly reject the idea of being made healthy by another people . . .

It has to be reckoned with that America will not contribute to the security of Europe against Russia forever. And therefore it seems to us the order of the hour finally to realize the community of interests for which far-sighted Englishmen and Germans of understanding have struggled for more than fifty years. . . .

It seems to us that the uniting of the Europeans into a European federation is called for. The goal of such an arrangement must be to safeguard Europe completely against any repetition of a European war. Any European war is sheer suicide. The time is ripe to translate this idealistic thought into reality, for the realistic situation supports the ideal.

We recommend a step-by-step procedure:

A European economic council should be permanently in session and concern itself first with removal of obstacles to trade, with setting up uniform traffic establishments, with a uniform rule for commerce, with removal of the customs borders, etc. When this process has gone far enough, common political organizations will be founded; for example:

a European ministry for economics;

European armed forces;

a European ministry for foreign affairs.

It will not be hard to reach an agreement over details. We are ready for every measure of cooperation – including a quicker method if it appears useful. In any case, the sole basis of a European community can be independence and freedom of decision for each of the nation-members.

Peace in Europe has to be secured by a process of arbitration, with all decisions based on common agreement . . .

Over and beyond a union of the European peoples, the world needs cooperation among all peoples. Without it, this or that great nation will be exposed to slumps in trade, to unemployment and poverty. In turn, this distress in one nation would have its effect on the others. Cooperation demands that, to begin with, each individual nation put its finances in order. For orderly state fiscal affairs are the first requisite of a stable currency. In turn, stable currencies are the sine qua non for restoration of world trade. In principle this trade should be as unhampered as possible, with particulars to be talked over and worked out. In order to speed this development, a world bank is needed. We noted the English and American suggestions in this field with great interest, and we consider them a good basis, on which we are certainly ready to cooperate.

As for Germany's future domestic political constitution, we can say some things with certainty, and can sketch others in outline.

That future state will guarantee the rights and freedom of the individual once more; it will restore freedom of conscience, freedom of thought; freedom of the press; it will be founded on democratic participation and control. But it also must take into account the lessons of the past. Democratic establishments can only be achieved by taking steps to restore a basis of law, to punish the criminals, and to restore the German people to political maturity. What top-level type of political organization Germany will have we cannot yet say. It is clear to us that only a monarchy within a parliamentary framework can grant inner tranquility to Germany with all possible speed and prepare it for its cooperative tasks. But we do not know how popular opinion will develop on this question.

The main aspect is that Germany should unequivocally do away with centralism, and restore the good, solid local administration of the communities, the administrative districts, and the states (*Länder*). Prussia will be merged with the *Reich*. The Prussian provinces will be no more. German states (*Länder*) will be formed that will have far-reaching self-government, as will the communities. The result will be that a central *Reich* government and central political representation will have only those functions that are indispensable for securing the cohesion of the *Reich* itself.

We are utterly convinced that the people of the world long for peace and for genuine tranquillity. Religious convictions in Germany have become enormously widened and deepened because of the suppression of such feelings in the last decade. The Christian faith and its teachings will remain our cornerstone and our guiding principle in all domestic and external political dealings. We consider it necessary that our foreign policy be founded on and harmonized with the Christian ethic.

4

Extracts from the Valkyrie Order of 26 May 1942, with its original intention of protection against an internal uprising, probably involving foreign workers in Germany, signed by Olbricht, representing General Fromm, Commander of the Reserve Army.

Head of Army Equipment and Commander of the Reserve Army, Berlin 26.5.1942 . . . Secret Command Matter Ref.: Valkyrie II . . .

General

In the event of surprise threat and other emergencies, the *readiness for action of the Reserve Army* or parts of it according to the situation for deployment locally, in the homeland or in border areas must be guaranteed. Preparations and execution have the password 'Valkyrie II' . . .

XI. *Secrecy.* The circle of those involved in carrying out the preparatory work is to be kept as small as possible. On no account should offices or individuals outside the Wehrmacht obtain knowledge of the intentions or preparations.

[signed]
By order.
Olbricht [handwritten signature].

Source: Bundesarchiv/Militärarchiv, Freiburg, RH12–21/8.

Extract from the Valkyrie Plan, with the preamble now amended to serve as the justification for an attempted coup d'état, produced by Colonel Henning von Tresckow between 7 September and 10 October 1943. This and related documents were recently discovered in Moscow. [Tresckow's plan envisaged the occupation of the headquarters in East Prussia not only of Hitler, but also of Himmler, Göring and Ribbentrop. Rapidly changing circumstances necessitated alterations in the plan over the coming months.]

Headquarters, [date, left open]

1) Treasonable elements in the SS and Party are attempting through exploiting the situation in the intense struggle on the eastern front to effect a stab in the back and to seize power for their own ends.

2) In order to establish peace, security and order, a military state of emergency is proclaimed and executive power handed to the Commander-in-Chief of the Wehrmacht . . .

Source: Peter Hoffmann, 'Oberst i.G. Henning von Tresckow und die Staatsstreichpläne im Jahr 1943', *Vierteljahrshefte für Zeitgeschichte*, Heft 2 (2007), p. 358.

5

Timetable for the Bendlerstraße group with orders prepared for the uprising

Little of the detailed logistical plan of a coup d'état, probably worked out, as the Security Police thought, by Stauffenberg's adjutant, Werner von Haeften, could be implemented as intended in the confused circumstances following the failed assassination attempt.

Time schedule

Commander replacement army	Corps Area Hq III

x – 1 day Valkyrie rehearsal (Order 1) at armoured troops school, Döberitz infantry school, Potsdam officer-candidates' school, Potsdam officers' school

x day (1) issue of basic orders to corps area Hq

(1) Basic order is delivered. General Olbricht informs chief of corps area Hq III

x time (2) Order to all parts of corps area Hq III

x time (2) advance order to Berlin Commandant (Order 2)

later (3) order to Berlin Commandant (Order 3)

x time	(4) advance order to commander of armoured troops school (Order 4)
later	(5) order to commander of armoured forces troops school (Order 5)
	(6) turnover by Berlin Commandant and armoured troops school to corps area Hq III

Order 1

Valkyrie rehearsal at the schools
x – 1 day to be issued.

Order 2

1. Order to the armed forces commander of Berlin (to be given out by telephone at x-time).

(1) Domestic unrest, state of martial law, executive power given to the army.

(2) Berlin guard battalion, immediately, with all available units, to armed forces garrison, Berlin headquarters, *Unter den Linden* 1.

(3) Berlin Commandant, with deputy chief of staff for operations and orderly officer, immediately, for receiving orders, to chief of army equipment, commander replacement army, *Bendlerstraße* 11–13.

(4) Send alarm to all units in Berlin garrison (Valkyrie, etc.) with priority to: (a) Spandau garrison, (b) arms and equipment school.

(5) 270 tons of motor-convoy capacity at Bernau is available for movement.

Order 3

2. Order to the armed forces garrison commander, Berlin (to be handed out to and discussed with commander personally).

(1) The situation is as follows . . .

(2) Berlin guard battalion into immediate action to blockade the Berlin government quarter: *Dorotheen, Friedrich, Koch, Anhalter, Saarland, Bellevue, Lenné* and *Hermann Göring* streets.

Mission: No person – including a minister of government – may enter or leave the blockaded district. In case of opposition, use of weapons. Sealing off of underground and district train stations. Other traffic to be diverted or to be moved empty through the blocked-off area. All persons in the blockaded area to remain indoors. The Propaganda Ministry at the *Wilhelmplatz* and the *SS* Main Office (*Albrechtstraße*) are particularly to be guarded.

Reich Minister Goebbels is to be arrested.

Commander is to send order to the garrison at once by telephone so that no time is lost.

(3) The blockade will be reinforced by two battalions of the armoured troops school, which will arrive immediately.

(4) Berlin Commandant himself receives further reinforcements by calling up Valkyrie and alarm units in his area (Spandau garrison, arms and equipment school).

Report on execution of blockade plan is to

be made to the commander of replacement army, chief of general army office and corps area Hq III, dept. I–A.

(5) The following points are to be occupied:

(a) Highest *Reich* authorities (enclosure 1).

First priority to I–a, 5–c,

Propaganda Ministry, *SS* Main Office (*Hermann-Göring-Straße, Albrechtstraße* and *Kaiserallee*),

Gau leadership in Berlin (*Voss-Straße*),

Hitler Youth leadership (*Kaiserdamm* 45),

Foreign Office,

Residences of *Reich* Minister (*Schwanenwerder* and *Lanke*).

(b) Communications installations (enclosure 2).

First priority:

Berlin telephone exchange (*Winterfeldstraße*),

Main telegraph office (*Oranienburgstraße*),

SS main exchange (*Albrechtstraße*),

Central Post Office (*Ringbahnstraße*).

(c) Newspaper and press (*Kochstraße*).

(6) The following are already occupied by other units of the corps area Hq command III: Tegel broadcasting station, radio tower and station building (*Masurenallee*).

These units are needed by corps area Hq III, and are to be made available by Berlin Commandant.

(7) Police are directed to cooperate with the army. Police will establish a blockade and control at the *Autobahn* ring.

(8) After arrival at post headquarters of sufficient troops and the assigned guidance officers and

officials, task forces are to be sent to the individual *Reich* authorities' offices (No. 5) to arrest the leading personalities. Signals officers are assigned to maintain communications.

(9) After the arrests, all persons without significance for the operation who are in the blockaded area are to be dismissed from it. Persons who need to pass the control points more than once are to be provided with passes by post headquarters. The blocked-off area may be left only at one point (for instance, *Unter den Linden* in the direction of the Palace).

(10) The commander of the army motor patrol service is subordinated to the Berlin armed forces' garrison headquarters.

(11) By truck from Brandenburg, 50 men of the Brandenburg division are supplied to the Berlin armed forces' garrison headquarters.

(12) *SS* units and Hermann Göring regiment.

(a) A task force under leadership of a general is dispatched to the commander of the Berlin *SS* garrison in order to arrange for the incorporation of the armoured *SS* into the army and to transmit order to that effect to the armoured *SS*.

(b) The Hermann Göring regiment in Tegel is to receive this order from the armed forces garrison headquarters: domestic unrest, Hermann Göring regiment to stay on the alert in its quarters. Commander with adjutant to the armed forces garrison headquarters, Berlin, *Unter den Linden* 1, to receive further orders.

(13) All important occurrences, successes and incidents are to be reported to the chief of army equipment, commander of replacement army, chief of general army office and corps area Hq III, Dept. I–A.

Order 4

Order to armored troops school (Krampnitz-Groß Glienicke)
(With x-time by telephone to commander of the armoured troops school, Colonel Gorn).

(1) Domestic unrest, state of martial law, executive power to the army.

(2) Commander of the armoured troops school with school's own three Valkyrie battalions and subordinated Valkyrie units of the officer candidates training courses of the infantry, Potsdam (one battalion with five companies) and the non-commissioned officers school, Potsdam (one battalion with three companies), proceed immediately by motor convoy to Berlin area *Tiergarten-Bendlerstraße*.

Commander, report before troops to chief of army equipment, commander of replacement army, Berlin W, *Bendlerstraße* 11.

(3) A strong combat unit (one armoured personnel carrier reconnaissance car company and one motorized infantry company) under energetic leadership is to take by surprise:
The broadcasting stations Königswusterhausen and Zeesen (near Königswusterhausen).

Resistance must be overcome by force of arms (at present, Zeesen is occupied by a company of the armoured *SS*). Political broadcasts may not be made. Broadcasting stations are to be held until the arrival of reinforcements. Occupation of the stations to be reported to corps area Hq III, Dept. I–A.

(4) 170 tons of motor vehicle convoy space from Kanin (24 kilometers southwest of Potsdam) are available.

Order 5

To commander of the armoured troops school (after his arrival at headquarters of chief of army equipment).

(1) Two battalions for reinforcement of the Berlin guard battalion (blockading government quarters) are subordinated to the armed forces garrison commander of Berlin.

(2) The bulk of the units under direction of commander of armoured troops school takes over protection of chief of army equipment, commander of the replacement army (*Bendler* block) and remains at disposal of corps area Hq III for flexible assignment.

(3) Telephone Dept. I–A, corps area Hq III.

(4) Reconnaissance to the south, to the barracks of the armed *SS* in Lichterfelde and Lankwitz.

(5) One company (if possible, armoured personal carrier) ready on call to meet commander and head of replacement army at Tempelhof Airport.

(6) One company with heavy arms remains ready as task force for dispatch to the SS garrison commander, Berlin.

Instruction for behaviour toward armoured SS.

(1) At the start, block off all roads of access to SS quarters. Bring heavy arms into position.

(2) Prepare raiding patrols for sudden armed intervention.

(3) Send energetic officer with escort officer to the main guard, where he is to ask for the senior SS leader present (at night, the duty officer). If possible, do not enter the building. Accompanying messengers remain at barracks entrance and maintain visual contact with the surrounding troops.

(4) The following shall be announced to the SS leader: The *Führer* is dead. A small clique of unscrupulous non-combatant party leaders has attempted a coup d'état. A state of martial law has been proclaimed, and the executive power has been handed over to the corps area Hq commanders.

With immediate effect, the armoured SS is to be merged with the army and is subordinated to the corps area headquarters commanders. Their troops are to remain in barracks until arrival of further orders and to refrain from action. Unless this order is carried out, the troops that have surrounded their quarters and are ready to fire with heavy arms will use any means to enforce the order. I must ask you to give the necessary orders, from here, in my presence.

(5) In case of refusal or resistance, the *SS* leader must be shot, the guard disarmed and the entire *SS* unit must be forced to lay down its weapons.

(6) If the *SS* units have already been alerted and are marching off, they are to be halted and made to return to barracks, by use of the aforesaid notification. At the least sign of resistance, there must be ruthless recourse to arms.

(7) When the *SS* has carried out the order, your own troops remain in front of the barracks until receipt of instructions from corps area Hq III, with which liaison is to be maintained; or until the incorporation of the *SS* into the army has been officially confirmed.

6

SS Report on the Conspiracy, 26 July 1944

In less than a week, the Special Commission from within the Security Police set up to investigate the plot against Hitler was able to provide this detailed reconstruction of events immediately before and after the assassination attempt.

Reich Chief Security Office – IV –
Special Commission for July 20, 1944

Berlin, July 26, 1944

Report on the plot against the *Führer* of July 20, 1944.

On July 20, 1944, at about 12:50 P.M., a detonation occurred in the '*Wolfsschanze*,' Restricted Area A, visitors' barracks, during the briefing session. The *Führer* suffered only slight injuries, although in the immediate vicinity of the centre of the explosion . . .

II.

Immediately after plot became known, *Reich* Leader *SS* appointed special commission of *Reich* Main Security Office for investigation of the attempt. Investigations began on the same day.

Reich Leader *SS* noted during detailing of circumstances that perpetrator of attempt was presumably Graf von Stauffenberg, colonel, chief of staff at office of commander of replacement army. He had been present at briefing session, then withdrew without notice before the explosion. Immediately afterward he went to Berlin by plane.

III.

Specific place of the assassination attempt was conference room where daily briefing sessions took place, about 40 feet long and 15 feet wide. In the centre of the room stands a large map table; to the left, writing desk and radio-phonograph. Room and all furnishings heavily damaged. To the right of entrance, 22-inch hole in floor. For wider radius, floor pressed in and charred. Points of impact of metal fragments not detectable, but wood splinters and leather fragments are impacted into fibre-board walls.

Bomb crater shows that explosion occurred above surface of floor. Reconstituted fragments of the right section of three sections of table show clearly the direction of the pressure wave. It is indicated in photographs and sketches.

Lower pressure wave from detonation continued through cavities under floor through the entire barracks and caused minor damage to a brick and cement framework of the barracks, particularly by a buckling up-Ward of the floor. Upper pressure wave destroyed conference room to a large extent and found exit through window and door, as well as through partition wall. Very minute sifting of mass of rubble has led to discovery of extremely small leather and metal fragments, obviously from a brief-case; of pieces of sheet metal and two compression springs from English chemical-mechanical time-fuse firing pins; also, part of flat iron pliers. Other material discovered has no obvious connection with the explosive.

Along the road leading from south exit to airport, an engineer search unit has found: a 975-g. lump of explosive, with priming chambers of 20 g. each and one English chemical-mechanical time-fuse firing pin, connected to English detonator cap, and set for 30-minute delay. Explosive was wrapped in brown wrapping paper.

Medical report: Injuries and contusions attributed solely to pressure of blast. Additionally, considerable burns. In several wounds, fragments of wood, straw, and, presumably, tattered leather. X-ray photographs reveal in all only two small metal splinters, presumably from lock of brief-case.

IV.

Leather fragments that were discovered have been identified by witnesses as belonging to Stauffenberg's briefcase. Small parts of igniter found at place of explosion come from two igniters that are of same type as the two English chemical-mechanical time-fuse pins found along the road. As two compression springs from this type of time-fuse were found at place of explosion, the explosive charge must have contained two such igniters. The charge that was found along the road was also arranged for two igniters. Therefore the explosive that was used for the attempt was presumably of exactly the same kind as that which was found. According to report of explosive expert, the extent of damage at place of explosion corresponds to potential power of explosive that was discovered.

Driver of car that took Stauffenberg to airport observed that he threw an object out the window in the general area of the discovery, and driver has given an affidavit. Thus Stauffenberg's complicity has been objectively ascertained.

V.

As chief of staff under Colonel-General Fromm, Stauffenberg has repeatedly taken part in briefings in the *Führer*'s headquarters. Local situation therefore was known to him. He landed Rastenburg airport July 20,

1944, at 10:15 a.m. Major-General Stieff, chief organization department of army high command, and 1st Lt.
von Haeften, aide-de-camp of Stauffenberg, arrived at
the same time. Stauffenberg went directly to '*Wolfsschanze*,' Stieff to army high command quarters, von
Haeften first with Stieff, was later to meet Stauffenberg
at '*Wolfsschanze*.'

Stauffenberg breakfasted in officers' mess with commander, until called to scheduled talk with General
Buhle. General von Thadden, chief of staff at commander of military district I, Königsberg, also partici-
pated in this meeting.

Afterward, Buhle, von Thadden and Stauffenberg
went to a conference with Field-Marshal Keitel.

Throughout the whole time, Stauffenberg kept his
brief-case with him. When all persons mentioned were
ready to go to briefing session from Keitel's bunker at
12:30 p.m., Stauffenberg went to a room next-door with
his brief-case for a short time, so that the other gentlemen
had to wait for him. Presumably while there he released
the time-fuses by pushing them in, presumably with the
help of pair of flat pliers; as his right hand and two
fingers of his left hand were missing, pushing in of the
time-fuses without such aid would have been difficult
for him. In conference room, Stauffenberg was reported
to the *Führer* as having been summoned to the session,
and was greeted by the *Führer*. After that, Stauffenberg
went to the map table, putting brief-case under table, to
the right of Colonel Brandt. After a short time, he left
the briefing room and also left Restricted Area A.

Stauffenberg was already missed before the explosion,

as he was to have provided some information in the briefing session. General Buhle looked for him. After the detonation, the telephone operator, Sgt. Adam, reported that he had seen Stauffenberg leave shortly after start of briefing session. Presumably latter was perpetrator of explosion, said sergeant.

From further interrogations and investigations, the following emerged: At about noon, General Fellgiebel, commissioner general for signals system, appeared at office of armed forces signals officer in *Führer* headquarters (Lieut. Col. Sander) in order to discuss several official matters with him. First Fellgiebel and Sander went together to Lieut. Col. Waizenegger of General Jodl's staff, because of various radio matters. Later Fellgiebel and Sander returned to the latter's office in *Bunker 88*.

At about 12:30 p. m., they noted that Field-Marshal Keitel, accompanied by Stauffenberg and others, was headed for the briefing session.

In order to make sure that Stauffenberg would come to General Fellgiebel after the briefing session, Sander telephoned Sgt. Adam that he should ask Stauffenberg to come to *Bunker 88* after the briefing.

Shortly after that, 1st Lt. von Haeften appeared in Sander's study and asked Fellgiebel for help in procuring a car, as Colonel Stauffenberg had to leave immediately. Accordingly, Sander telephoned the command post to request a car. At that time he was asked by the command post to remind Stauffenberg that he was expected for lunch with the commander, Lieut. Col. Streve, with General von Thadden also to be present.

While this phone conversation was continuing, Stauffenberg had looked into the room and announced himself to General Fellgiebel as being ready for their talk. Then Fellgiebel and Stauffenberg went out in front of the bunker and discussed fortifications in the East. Sander joined them and reported that a car was coming, adding that Stauffenberg was expected for lunch with the commander. Thereupon Stauffenberg told Lieut. Col. Sander that first he had to go back to the briefing session once more, and would then come to lunch. He also pointed out that he had a car at his disposal. When Sander had informed headquarters accordingly, and returned to the front of the bunker, the detonation occurred. At that moment Sander noted a very nervous demeanour on the part of Stauffenberg. In reply to Fellgiebel's perplexed question as to what was the matter, Sander declared, without thinking seriously about the matter, that occasionally someone fired a gun, or a mine went off.

Then Stauffenberg said he was not going back to the briefing session, but instead would go to the lunch with Lieut. Col. Streve. He drove away with von Haeften, actually in order to go to the airfield.

What took place in the visitors' barracks was partially noted by the Guardpost 1, so that the lieutenant on duty ordered the barriers closed. Accordingly, Stauffenberg was halted by the guard. He told the guard commander that he must get to the airfield urgently. As his pass was in order and additionally as he was known to the guard commander, the latter let him pass; particularly as the general alarm had not yet been sounded, but came only

1½ minutes later. At the outer southern guardpost, Stauffenberg was halted again. He went to the guard commander, Sgt. Kolbe, whom he told that he had by all means to get to the airport at once. Instead of being persuaded, Kolbe pointed out the closed barriers. Then Kolbe telephoned headquarters, on Stauffenberg's request, and got in touch with the adjutant, von Möllendorf, cavalry captain, in the absence of the commander, who was at the place of the explosion. Stauffenberg told Möllendorf that he had received the commander's permission to leave the security area, and that he had to fly by 1:15 p.m. at all events. The adjutant, who did not know the reason for the alarm that had been sounded, while he did know that Colonel Stauffenberg was authorized to be at the '*Wolfsschanze*,' agreed, on the strength of what Stauffenberg told him, to the colonel's departure, and confirmed his agreement on the telephone to Sgt. Kolbe.

In this situation, it is to be taken into consideration that:

1. The alarm is sounded rather frequently.
2. Stauffenberg's papers were in order.
3. Since Stauffenberg was known as a seriously disabled fighting man and an officer in excellent standing, von Möllendorf had no reason at first to be suspicious.

Stauffenberg also then passed the southern guard-post, and took off at 13:15 p.m. from Rastenburg airport for Berlin-Rangsdorf. Inquiry as to the origin of the plan has revealed that it was provided for Stauffenberg by order of General Wagner, army Quartermaster General, by arrangement with the 1st air liaison wing (2), Berlin, from Lötzen airport. The plane was scheduled in any case to go to Berlin.

VI.

In the light of the above report, the circumstances of the attempted assassination, and the arrival and departure of the perpetrator, can be considered as having been objectively determined.

It cannot be concluded that security measures existing as a safeguard against such attempts broke down in this instance; for the possibility that a general staff officer summoned to a briefing session would lend himself to such a crime had not been reckoned with.

The incident does, however, require consideration of the future security measures to be taken for the protection of the *Führer* in any circumstances. Accordingly, proposals with regard to security measures will be submitted separately, by agreement with the *Reich* Main Security Office.

7

Teletype Messages from Witzleben and Stauffenberg at Bendlerstraße, 20 July 1944

These were the first – by Witzleben, the designated military commander-in-chief of the post-Hitler regime, and by Stauffenberg (under Fromm's name) – of a series of orders dispatched by the leaders of the coup following Stauffenberg's return from Führer Headquarters, though with rapidly diminishing effectiveness once Hitler's survival became known.

Teletype message 1

– FRR – HOKW 02150 20. 7. 44, 16.45
FRR to corps area Hq XII – secret –
Domestic unrest.

I. An unscrupulous clique of non-combat party leaders has tried to exploit the situation to stab the deeply-committed front in the back, and to seize power for selfish purposes.

II. In this hour of highest danger, the *Reich* government has in order to maintain law and order proclaimed a state of martial law, and has at the same time delegated supreme executive power of the armed forces to me.

III. Accordingly I order the following.

1. I transfer the executive power – with the right of delegation to the territorial commanders – in the Homeland War Zone to the commander of the replacement army, appointing him at the same time commander-in-chief in the Homeland War Zone.

In the occupied West areas, to the commander-in-chief West (commander-in-chief of army group D), in Italy to the commander-in-chief Southwest (commander-in-chief of army group C), in the Southeast area to the commander-in-chief Southeast (commander-in-chief of army group F), in the occupied East areas to the commanders-in-chief of army groups South Ukraine, North Ukraine, Middle, North and the armed forces commander *Ostland* for their respective command areas; in Denmark and in Norway, to the commanders of the armed forces.

2. To the holders of executive power are subordinated:

(a) All offices and units of the armed forces, including the armoured *SS*, the *Reich* Labour Service and the *Organisation Todt*, that are within their command area.

(b) All public authorities (of the *Reich*, the states and the communities), in particular the entire police forces, including forces for keeping order, for security, for administration.

(c) All office-holders and formations of the National Socialist party and its affiliated units.

(d) Transport and supply operations.

3. The entire armoured *SS* is incorporated into the army, with this order to take effect immediately.

4. The holders of executive power are responsible for maintenance of order and public safety. In particular they are charged with:

(a) Securing the signals installations.

(b) The elimination of the *SD*. Any resistance to the military executive power must be ruthlessly broken.

5. In this hour of highest danger for the fatherland, solidarity of the armed forces and maintenance of full discipline is the highest order.

Therefore I charge all commanders in the army, the navy and the air force with supporting the bearers of executive power in carrying out their difficult task with all means at their disposal, and with ensuring obedience of their orders by subordinate offices. The German soldier is facing a historic task. On his determination and bearing will depend whether Germany is to be saved.

The same responsibilities apply to all territorial commanders, the high command of the branches of the armed forces and the immediately subordinate command authorities of the army, navy and air force.

The commander-in-chief of the armed forces.

signed: v. Witzleben, Field-Marshal

Teletype message 2

– Kr – HOKW 02155 20 July 1944, 18:00
To Corps areas Hq I–XIII, XVII, XVIII, XX, XXI, corps area Hq,
Governor-General, Bohemia-Moravia. Secret!

I. Under the authority given to me by the commander-in-chief of the armed forces, I transfer the executive power in the corps areas to the deputy commanding generals and corps area commanders. Together with the executive power, the authority of the *Reich* defence commissioners passes over to the corps area commanders.

II. The following immediate measures are to be taken: (a) Signals installations: The principal buildings and installations of the post and armed forces signals network (including radio installations) are to be made militarily secure. The forces assigned to this task must be strong enough to prevent interference and sabotage. Principal signals installations are to be occupied by officers These in particular are to be made secure: amplifying stations, communications exchanges of the army operations network, high-power transmitters (broadcasting stations), telephone and telegraph offices insofar as major telephone lines run through them, amplifier and battery rooms, antennas, emergency power supplies and operating rooms. The communication network of the railway is to be protected in agreement with the transport offices.

Radio network is to kept operative from own resources.

(b) Arrests: The following are to be removed from their posts without delay and are to be held in individual arrest: all regional (*Gau*) leaders, *Reich* governors' ministers, senior presidents, police presidents, higher *SS* and police leaders, *Gestapo* leaders and chief of *SS* officers, chief of propaganda offices and area leaders. Exceptions are to be ordered by me.

(c) Concentration camps: The concentration camps are to be occupied speedily, the camp commanders arrested, the guards disarmed and confined to barracks. The political prisoners are to be informed that they must abstain from all demonstrations and individual measures until their discharge.

(d) Armoured *SS*: If doubts exist as to the obedience of leaders of armoured *SS* units or of senior officers of the armoured *SS*, or if they seem unsuitable for further command, they are to be taken into protective custody and replaced by officers of the army. Units of the armoured *SS* whose unlimited obedience is in doubt are to be disarmed ruthlessly. This is to be accomplished energetically with superior forces, to avoid bloodshed as far as possible.

(e) Police: The offices of the *Gestapo* and of the *SD* are to be occupied. Regular police are to be utilized for relief of the armed forces.

Police orders are to be issued through the chief of German police via police command.

(f) Navy and air force: Connection is to be established with commanders of navy and air force. Common action is to be achieved.

III. For the administration of all political matters that arise under the state of martial law, I appoint a political commissioner for each corps area. Until further notice he is to discharge the tasks of the chief of administration. He is to advise the commander of the corps area in all political matters.

IV. The administrative office of the Commander-in-Chief of the Homeland War Zone is the Homeland Operations Staff. It will send a liaison officer to the corps area commanders for the purpose of mutual information about the situation and intentions..

V. No arbitrary actions or actions based on vengeance are to be tolerated in the exercise of the executive power. The population must be made aware that the executive power distances itself from the arbitrary methods of the previous rulers.

The Commander-in-Chief in the Homeland War Zone No. 32 160/44, secret.

signed: Fromm, Colonel-General.
Graf Stauffenberg, Colonel.

8

Speech by Hitler, 21 July 1944, at about 1 a.m.

The speech aimed to emphasise to the German people not only that Hitler was alive and well, but that Providence had saved him to continue to lead his country, and – which was untrue – that it was only 'a very small clique' of officers who had stood against him and would now be 'ruthlessly exterminated'.

Führer headquarters, July 20, 1944
The *Führer* delivered the following address tonight to the German people over the German radio network:

My comrades, the men and women of the German people!

I don't know how many times it is by now that an assassination has been planned and attempted against me. But I am talking to you today for two reasons:

1. so that you can hear my voice and know that I am unhurt and well;

2. but also so that you may know the details of a crime that is without equal in German history.

A tiny clique of ambitious, unconscionable and at the

same time criminal, stupid officers has forged a plot to eliminate me and at the same time to eradicate with me the staff practically of the German armed forces' leadership.

The bomb that was planted by Colonel Graf von Stauffenberg exploded two metres from my right side. It very seriously wounded a number of my valuable staff members. One of them has died. I myself am absolutely unhurt, except for very light scratches, bruises and burns. I interpret this as a confirmation of the orde of Providence that I continue to pursue the goal of my life, as I have done up to now. For I may solemnly state before the whole nation that since the day I moved into Wilhelmstraße I have had only one thought: to do my duty according to my best understanding and my conscience. Since it became clear to me that the war was inevitable and could no longer be put off, I have in fact known nothing but worry and work and lived through countless days and sleepless nights only for my people.

At an hour in which the German armies are committed to the hardest fighting, a small group existed in Germany – as one did in Italy – that believed it could deliver a stab in the back as in the year 1918. But this time the conspirators have very much deceived themselves. The allegation by these usurpers that I am no longer alive is contradicted by this very moment in which I speak to you, my dear comrades. The circle of these conspirators is a very small one. It has nothing to do with the German armed forces, and particularly not with the German army. It is a tiny gang of criminal elements who will now be ruthlessly exterminated.

Therefore I order at this moment:

1. that no civilian authority has to take any order from any office that these usurpers seek to control,

2. that no military authority, no troop leader, no soldier, has to obey any order of these usurpers; that, on the contrary, everybody is obliged either to arrest the transmitter or giver of such an order at once, or, in case of resistance, to do away with him immediately.

So as finally to create order, I have appointed *Reichsminister* Himmler as commander of the Home Army. I have called Colonel-General Guderian into the general staff in order to take the place of the chief of the general staff who has currently retired because of illness. I have assigned a second proven leader of the East front as his assistant.

Nothing is changed in any other office of the *Reich*. I am convinced that with the disappearance of this tiny clique of traitors and conspirators we are finally creating the atmosphere at the rear, in the homeland, that the fighters at the front need. For it is unthinkable that at the front hundreds of thousands and millions of good men should give their all while a small gang of ambitious and miserable creatures here at home tries to permanently circumvent this attitude. This time we are going to settle accounts as we National Socialists are used to doing it.

I am convinced that every decent officer, every brave soldier, will understand that, in this hour.

Perhaps only a few today can imagine what fate would have befallen Germany if the plot had succeeded. I thank Providence and my creator, and not because he has preserved me. My life is only worry, only work for my people. But I thank him, rather because he has made it possible for me to go on carrying these worries, and to pursue my work as well as I can, before my conscience.

Every German, regardless of who he is, has the duty of ruthlessly countering these elements, either to arrest them immediately or, if they offer resistance in any form, do away with them straightaway. Orders have been issued to all troops. They will be carried out blindly, with the obedience that the German army knows.

I may joyfully greet you in particular once more, my old battle comrades, in that it was granted to me again to escape a destiny that had nothing terrible in it for me, but that would have brought horror for the German people.

I also see in this an omen from Providence that I must carry on my work, and therefore I shall carry it on.

9

Jodl's address, 24 July 1944

In his speech to a number of officers in the Operations Staff, which he led, General Jodl (1890–1946), Hitler's chief military adviser, admitted that the plot had more extensive backing than had initially been thought and portrayed it as a day of ignominy even worse than 9 November 1918 – the day of the revolution at the end of the First World War that was etched on the pysche of the Nazi leadership.

Führer headquarters, July 25, 1944
Speech of the chief of the armed forces operations staff, General Jodl, to the officers and officials of the armed forces operations staff, in the officers' home of Restricted Area II, on July 24, 1944, 7:30 p.m.

The 20th of July was the blackest day that German history has seen up to now, and perhaps will remain so for all future time. Previously it had been November 9, 1918. But compared with what has happened just now, November 9 was almost a day of honour. For, as an excuse for November 9, one can argue that a portion of the German people who had been educated against the state and stood in no connection with it proceeded to a revolution. Even in respect to the Italian treason of last year, it can be asserted that the leading personalities were carrying out an order of the head of state. Thus these previous occasions are not comparable with the far more foul deed of July 20. It was carried out by officers who were bound by their oath of allegiance, who went in and out of the *Führer* headquarters constantly, were permitted to shake hands with the *Führer*, and had been promoted by him. Except in Russia and Mexico, a similar thing has probably never happened before in the whole world. It remains unique in its monstrosity. Could the conspirators, who were close to the Jesuits, quote the maxim, 'The end justifies the means?' If they were ready to do that, then they would only prove their vast stupidity, and their smallness of vision. For how did they plan to be useful to their people? 1918 has already shown what it means to hope for a cheap peace by getting rid of the regime . . .

It is incomprehensibly short-sighted to expect that a putsch will make possible an approach to the Anglo-Saxons, when the latter cannot hold their position vis-à-vis the Soviets. If the plot had succeeded, then after some fighting order might have been restored in the interior. But the danger was that in the meantime the front would have broken up.

So much for the way the events appear from the standpoints of politics and discipline. The human aspect is even more sad. One would like to sink into the ground from shame. Since 1918, the once firmly united officers' corps, harmonious within its ranks, has simply no longer existed. In the time that it did exist, from the founding of the *Reich* onward, I am sure it never experienced a single case of high treason and felony. . . .

It has emerged that the action spread farther then was indicated by the *Führer* in his speech. Persons who do not belong to the armed forces were also involved. But now a general reckoning will be made, and carried through 100 per cent. Compassion is out of place, and the time for lukewarm followers is past. Ruthless hatred for all those who resist! That is what I myself feel. . . .

After everything rotten has been weeded out, the question is how to unite the remaining parts. We must acknowledge that the people has maintained a better attitude than those officers, even though the population has had to suffer more than the perpetrators of the plot.

Now the will to resist the enemy has blazed up brightly. . . . Thus we are strengthened in the hope that we will weather this crisis, than which a worse one cannot be imagined. I cherish the expectation that among all the officers whom I look in the eye, there will not be a single lukewarm person. I am convinced that we shall get through this situation. But even if luck should be against us, then we would have to determine to gather around the *Führer* with our weapons at the last, so that we may be justified before posterity. For us older ones, this is easier than for the younger among us. But that does not alter the fact that we must acquit ourselves with honour before history and posterity.

10

Extracts from the trials before the People's Court

These extracts, though brief, suffice to convey something of the tone of the Court proceedings and the way in which the President of the People's Court, Roland Freisler (1893–1945) attempted to denigrate and humiliate the accused.

From the trial of Graf Yorck von Wartenburg.

Yorck: Mr President! I have already stated that in view of the development that has been taken by the National Socialist ideology, I did –

Freisler (interrupting): – did not agree! To state it exactly, you told him: regarding the Jewish question, the extermination of the Jews did not suit you; the National Socialis concept of justice did not suit you.

Yorck: The essential point is the connection between all these questions, the claim by the state of total power over the citizen, with the elimination of his religious and moral obligations toward God.

Freisler: Tell me, where has National Socialism eliminated the moral obligation of a German? National

Socialism has made the moral obligations of a German, of the German man, of the German woman, infinitely more healthy, has infinitely deepened them. I have never heard before that it had eliminated moral obligations. And as for religion there National Socialism is very modest. It says: please take care of that as you wish, but only stay in the other world with your demands, church. For the souls, after all, will do their fluttering around in the other world. Here on earth our present life counts Otherwise the church could concern itself with politics. So what you say is at least quite distorted; it makes no sense.

Yorck: I wanted to give this simply as an explanation.

Freisler: Furthermore, insofar as the National Socialist concept of justice is concerned I can say, as a person who has been right in the middle of jurisprudence for many years, that our concept of law has also both theoretically and practically undergone an enormous deepening. The justice of our people has experienced an enormous revival and intensification . . . What you have said remains enigmatic. But you say: I did not agree. Now I ask you: if Stauffenberg asked you for your word of honour, and you listened to a thing like that, what kind of thoughts went on in your mind? Can such a word of honour be valid?

Yorck: I feel bound by it, Mr President.

Freisler: This is indeed a sign that your attitude is an absolutely anarchistic one.

Yorck: I would not express it exactly that way.

Freisler: But I believe that that is the clear and correct way of describing it. For it is anarchy if everyone can create a justice of freedom of action in the community, just by his own saying so. The general law of action in our community calls for combating and destroying treason against public, *Führer* and *Reich*, under any circumstances. If you make yourself the law, if you say 'When I give my word of honour, then I may not participate,' then this is an anarchistic principle that you have. You may call it something else . . .

During the trial of Graf Schwerin von Schwanenfeld before the People's Court in August 1944, Freisler turned to Graf Schwerin with the following question: You must have had special experience with the campaign in Poland. Were you not particularly much in action in West Prussia?

Graf Schwerin: Yes.

Freisler: In other words, you were privileged to liberate your own homeland, as a soldier of our *Führer*.

Graf Schwerin: Mr President, the political experiences that I underwent personally resulted in several kinds of difficulties for me. I worked for Germanism (*Deutschtum*) for a very long time in Poland, and during that time I experienced a back-and-forth-attitude toward the Poles. That is a –

Freisler: In any case, is the back-and-forth something that you can blame National Socialism for?

Graf Schwerin: I thought of the many murders –

Freisler: Murders?

Graf Schwerin: At home and abroad –

Freisler: You really are a low scoundrel. Are you breaking down under this rottenness? Yes or no, are you breaking down under it?

Graf Schwerin: Mr President!

Freisler: Yes or no, a clear answer!

Graf Schwerin: No.

Freisler: Nor can you break down any more. For you are nothing but a small heap of misery that has no respect for itself any longer.

11

A prison warden's description of the executions

Hitler's thirst for revenge against those who had plotted against him is reflected in this gruesome depiction of the execution scene, though whether Hitler indeed viewed the film that was made is not certain.

Imagine a room with a low ceiling and white-washed walls. Below the ceiling a rail was fixed. From it hung six big hooks, like those butchers use to hang their meat. In one corner stood a film camera. Reflecters cast a dazzling, blinding light, like that in a studio. In this strange, small room were the Prosecutor General of the *Reich*, the hangman with his two assistants, two camera technicians, and I myself with a second prison warden. At the wall there was a small table with a bottle of cognac and glasses for the witnesses of the execution.

The convicted men were led in. They were wearing their prison garb, and they were handcuffed. They were placed in a single row. Leering and making jokes, the hangman got busy. He was known in his circles for his 'humour.' No statement, no clergymen, no journalists.

One after another, all ten faced their turn. All showed the same courage. It took, in all, 25 minutes. The hangman wore a permanent leer, and made his jokes unceasingly. The camera worked uninterruptedly, for Hitler wanted to see and hear how his enemies had died. He was able to watch the proceedings that same evening in the *Reich* Chancellery. That was his own idea. He had had the executioner come to him, and had personally arranged the details of the procedure: 'I want them to be hanged, hung up like carcarsses of meat.' Those were his words.

1 2

Helmut Graf von Moltke's
last letter

*The depth of Moltke's Christian beliefs
(linked with a form of Socialism), which not
only sustained and motivated him, but gave
him the sense of moral superiority over
Nazism and its representatives who held
him in their clutches and would soon execute
him, is the dominant feature of this
extraordinary letter.*

January 11, 1945

. . . What was dramatic in the trial was, in the last analysis, the following: in the trial, no tangible accusations
could be borne out, and all of them were dropped. They
were forgotten. What the Third *Reich* is so afraid of
that it has to send five men – later it will be seven – to
death is in the end only this: a private individual, your
husband, of whom they have ascertained that he talked
with two clergymen of both confessions, with a Jesuit
and with a few bishops. They talked, without the intention of doing anything concrete – and that has been

152

ascertained – about things 'which belong exclusively to the competence of the *Führer*.' What was discussed was not by any chance questions of organization, not in any sense the organization of the *Reich* – all such charges were dropped in the course of trial, and Schulze* expressly said so in his summation ('. . . differs from all other cases in that the discussion made no mention of force or of any organization . . .'). Rather, the points of discussion were questions of the practical and ethical claims of Christianity. Nothing more; for that alone we are being convicted. Freisler said to me in one of his tirades: 'In one thing only are we and Christianity alike: We demand the whole person!' I do not know whether those sitting there got all that, for it was a kind of dialogue between Freisler and myself. A mental one, because I could not get in many words. During it, we recognized each other, through and through. Of the whole gang, only Freisler recognized me, and of the whole gang only he knows why he has to kill me. There was nothing of 'complicated person' or 'complicated thoughts' or 'ideology,' but simply: 'The fig-leaf is off.' But only for Herr Freisler. We talked with each other, so to say, in a vacuum. . . .

The decisive sentence in that trial was: 'Herr Graf, there is one thing Christianity and we National Socialists have in common, and only this one: We demand the whole human being.' Did he realize what he was saying there? Just think how miraculously God has prepared this unworthy vessel. At the moment in which the

* Prosecutor of the People's Court.

danger existed that I would be drawn into the active preparations for the putsch – for Stauffenberg came to Peter [Graf Yorck von Wartenburg] on the evening of January 19, 1944 – I was taken out, so that I am and remain free from any connection with the use of force. Then He implants in me that Socialist trait that frees me, a large landowner, from any suspicion of being a representative of interests. Then He humiliates me in a way I have never been humiliated before, so that I have had to lose all my pride, so that finally after 38 years I understand my sinfulness, so that I have learned to ask for His forgiveness and to entrust myself to His grace. Then He permits me to come to this place, where I could see you calmly and collectedly, and become free of thoughts of you and our small sons – that is, free of worrisome thoughts. Then He gives me the time and opportunity to put everything in order which could be put in order, so that all worldly thoughts can fall away. Then He lets me experience the pain of departure and the fear of death and the fear of hell in an unheard-of intensity; so that this, too, is past. Then He supplies me with faith, hope and love, with a richness of these things that is truly overflowing. . . .

My heart, my life is completed, and I can say of myself: he died old and satiated with life. This does not change the fact that I should like to live a little longer still, that I should like to accompany you for a stretch on this earth still. But a new order from God would be needed for that. The order for which God made me has been fulfilled. If He wants to give me still a new order, we shall learn about it. Accordingly, you can without hesitation make an effort to save my life in case I should survive today. Perhaps there will be another order.

I stop, for there is nothing more to say. I have not mentioned any one whom you should greet and embrace. You know yourself whom my directions to you are meant for. All our dear sayings are in my heart and in your heart. But I say to you, at the end, by virtue of the treasure which has been placed in me, and which fills this modest earthen vessel: May the grace of our Lord Jesus Christ and the love of God and the community of the Holy Spirit be with you all.

Amen.

13

Peter Graf Yorck von
Wartenburg's farewell letters
to his mother and his wife

*Yorck von Wartenburg (1904–44), Moltke's
closest associate in the Kreisau Circle,
expresses in this moving letter the altruistic
concern for a better Germany that had
underpinned his involvement in the
opposition to Hitler and, like Moltke, the
strength of his Christian belief that sustained
him as his execution loomed.*

From the good-bye letter to his mother

. . . The degree of inner misery that people like me had
to live in the past years is surely not understandable to
those who are completely enshrouded in their faith,
which I simply do not share. I may assure you that no
ambitious thought, no desire for power determined what
I did. It was merely feelings for my fatherland, my concern for my Germany as it has grown through the last
two thousand years, my effort on behalf of its internal
and external development, that led to my action. In that

way, I stand upright before my ancestors, my father, my brothers. Perhaps there will yet come a time that will judge us not as scoundrels but as prophets and patriots. That this wondrous call may give honour to God is my fervent prayer.

To his wife

. . . It seems that we are standing at the end of our beautiful and rich life together. For tomorrow the People's Court will sit in judgment on me and the others. I hear that the army has dismissed us. One can take away the garment, but not the spirit in which we acted. And in that spirit I feel close to fathers, brothers and comrades. . .

. . . I hope my death will be accepted as atonement for all my sins, and as an expiatory sacrifice for all that we carry together. By the sacrifice, our time's distance from God may be shortened by some small measure. For my part, I am dying for the fatherland. Although the outward appearance is most inglorious – yes, disgraceful – I walk this last way upright and erect; and I only hope that you do not see arrogance and delusion in this attitude. We want to kindle the torch of life; a sea of flames surrounds us – what a fire!

Index

PENGUIN HISTORY

HITLER 1889–1936: HUBRIS
IAN KERSHAW

'Magnificent ... the first of a two-volume biography which it is hard to believe
will ever be superseded' Niall Ferguson, *Evening Standard*

'The Hitler biography for the 21st century ... cool, judicious, factually reliable
and intelligently argued' Richard Evans, *Sunday Telegraph*

'Supersedes all previous accounts. It is the sort of masterly biography that only a
first-rate historian can write' David Cannadine, *Observer*, Books of the Year

'His analysis of Hitler's extraordinary character has the fascination of a novel, but
he places his struggle and the rise in the context of meticulously researched
history ... Deeply disturbing. Unforgettable' A. N. Wilson, *Daily Mail*

HITLER 1936–1945: NEMESIS
IAN KERSHAW

WINNER OF THE WOLFSON LITERARY AWARD FOR HISTORY

'I cannot imagine a better biography of this great tyrant emerging for a long
while' Jeremy Paxman, *Financial Times*

'An achievement of the very highest order ... Kershaw communicates a genuine
sense of tension as Hitler embarked on ever-riskier stratagems, bringing a fresh
eye to the over-familiar diplomatic or military story ... a marvellous book'
Michael Burleigh, *Financial Times*

'Extraordinarily convincing ... I do not know any other Hitler biography that so
coolly, factually and devastatingly presents the phenomena of "obedience" and
charisma' Gitta Sereny, *The Times*

PENGUIN HISTORY

FATEFUL CHOICES
IAN KERSHAW

'Powerfully argued ... important ... this book actually alters our perspective of the
Second World War' Andrew Roberts

In 1940 the world was on a knife-edge.

The hurricane of events that marked the opening of the Second World War
meant that anything could happen. For the aggressors there was no limit to their
ambitions; for their victims a new Dark Age beckoned. Over the coming months
their fates would be determined. In Fateful Choices Ian Kershaw re-creates the ten
critical decisions taken between May 1940, when Britain chose not to surrender,
and December 1941, when Hitler decided to destroy Europe's Jews, showing how
these choices would recast the entire course of history.

'A compelling re-examination of the conflict ... Kershaw displays here those
same qualities of scholarly rigour, careful argument and sound judgement that he
brought to bear so successfully in his life of Hitler' Richard Overy

'How fortunate that it is Ian Kershaw bringing his immense knowledge and
clarity of thought to the task ... brilliantly explained ... an immensely wise book'
Anthony Beevor